The middle years of the twentieth century marked a particularly intense time of crisis and change in European society. During this period (1930-1950), a broad intellectual and spiritual movement arose within the European Catholic community, largely in response to the secularism that lay at the core of the crisis. The movement drew inspiration from earlier theologians and philosophers such as Möhler, Newman, Gardeil, Rousselot, and Blondel, as well as from men of letters like Charles Péguy and Paul Claudel.

The group of academic theologians included in the movement extended into Belgium and Germany, in the work of men like Emile Mersch, Dom Odo Casel, Romano Guardini, and Karl Adam. But above all the theological activity during this period centered in France. Led principally by the Jesuits at Fourviére and the Dominicans at Le Saulchoir, the French revival included many of the greatest names in twentieth-century Catholic thought: Henri de Lubac, Jean Daniélou, Yves Congar, Marie-Dominique Chenu, Louis Bouyer, and, in association, Hans Urs von Balthasar.

It is not true — as subsequent folklore has it — that those theologians represented any sort of self-conscious "school": indeed, the differences among them, for example, between Fourviére and Saulchoir, were important. At the same time, most of them were united in the double conviction that theology had to speak to the present situation, and that the condition for doing so faithfully lay in a recovery of the Church's past. In other words, they saw clearly that the first step in what later came to be known as *aggiornamento* had to be *ressourcement* — a rediscovery of the riches of the whole of the Church's two-thousand-year tradition. According to de Lubac, for example, all of his own works as well as the entire *Sources chrétiennes* collection are based on the presupposition that "the renewal of Christian vitality is linked at least partially to a renewed exploration of the periods and of the works where the Christian tradition is expressed with particular intensity."

In sum, for the *ressourcement* theologians theology involved a "return to the sources" of Christian faith, for the purpose of drawing out the meaning and significance of these sources for the critical questions of our time. What these theologians sought was a spiritual and intellectual communion with Christianity in its most vital moments as transmitted to us in its classic texts, a communion that would nourish, invigorate, and rejuvenate twentieth-century Catholicism.

The *ressourcement* movement bore great fruit in the documents of the Second Vatican Council and has deeply influenced the work of Pope John Paul II.

The present series is rooted in this renewal of theology. The series thus understands *ressourcement* as revitalization: a return to the sources, for the purpose of developing a theology that will truly meet the challenges of our time. Some of the features of the series, then, are a return to classical (patristic-mediaeval) sources and a dialogue with contemporary Western culture, particularly in terms of problems associated with the Enlightenment, modernity, and liberalism.

The series publishes out-of-print or as yet untranslated studies by earlier authors associated with the *ressourcement* movement. The series also publishes works by contemporary authors sharing in the aim and spirit of this earlier movement. This will include any works in theology, philosophy, history, literature, and the arts that give renewed expression to Catholic sensibility.

The editor of the Ressourcement series, David L. Schindler, is Gagnon Professor of Fundamental Theology and dean at the John Paul II Institute in Washington, D.C., and editor of the North American edition of *Communio: International Catholic Review,* a federation of journals in thirteen countries founded in Europe in 1972 by Hans Urs von Balthasar, Jean Daniélou, Henri de Lubac, Joseph Ratzinger, and others.

RETRIEVAL & RENEWAL

IN CATHOLIC THOUGHT

VOLUMES PUBLISHED

The Portal of the Mystery of Hope
Charles Péguy

In the Beginning:
A Catholic Understanding of the Story of Creation and the Fall
Cardinal Joseph Ratzinger

In the Fire of the Burning Bush:
An Initiation to the Spiritual Life
Marko Ivan Rupnik

Hans Urs von Balthasar: A Theological Style
Angelo Scola

In the Fire of the Burning Bush

AN INITIATION TO THE SPIRITUAL LIFE

Marko Ivan Rupnik

Translated by

Susan Dawson Vásquez

WILLIAM B. EERDMANS PUBLISHING COMPANY
GRAND RAPIDS, MICHIGAN / CAMBRIDGE, U.K.

Wm. B. Eerdmans Publishing Co.
255 Jefferson Ave. S.E., Grand Rapids, Michigan 49503 /
P.O. Box 163, Cambridge CB3 9PU U.K.
www.eerdmans.com

Printed in the United States of America

09 08 07 06 05 04   7 6 5 4 3 2 1

Library of Congress Cataloging-in-Publication Data

Rupnik, Marko Ivan, 1954-
[Spritual life. English]
In the fire of the burning bush: an initiation to the spiritual life /
Marko Ivan Rupnik; translated by Susan Dawson Vásquez.
p.   cm.   — (Ressourcement)
Includes bibliographical references.
Contents: The spiritual life — Spiritual fatherhood.
ISBN 0-8028-2832-9
1. Spiritual life — Christianity.
I. Rupnik, Marko Ivan, 1954-   Spiritual fatherhood. English.
II. Title: Spiritual fatherhood.   III. Title.
IV. Ressourcement (Grand Rapids, Mich.)

BV4501.3.R868   2004
248.4'82 — dc22

2004053280

The two essays presented in this book are re-edited texts that originally appeared in Tomáš Špidlík, Maria Campatelli, et al., *Lezioni sulla Divinoumanità* (Lessons on Divine-Humanity) (Rome: Lipa, 1995) and in Tomaš Špidlík, Sergio Rendina, et al., *In colloquio: Alla scoperta della paternità spirituale* (In Conversation: In Search of Spiritual Paternity) (Rome: Lipa, 1995). It has been decided to maintain the original structure of their first publications that, although causing a few repetitions between the two parts, nevertheless does not disrupt the unity of this volume and responds to our readers' requests.

The Scripture quotations in this publication are from the New Revised Standard Version of the Bible, copyright © 1989 by the Division of Christian Education of the National Council of Churches of Christ in the U.S.A. Used by permission. All rights reserved.

Contents

CONTENTS

SPIRITUAL FATHERHOOD

A Majestic Path for Personal Wholeness

Foreword

ASKED TO DESCRIBE THEIR LIVES, people on the brink of despair might say something like this: "It's a trek through the desert." Today, this sort of phrase sounds a pessimistic note, but, in the biblical context, the same words connote hope and joy. What accounts for this difference? In the first case, we hear the sighing of men and women who feel lost in illusion and emptiness. But for Moses and his people, the desert was the mysterious path to the Promised Land, a path whose first steps were lit up by the burning bush, a path that was marked by a decisive encounter with the only One who can rightfully say, "I am, I am here (cf. Exod. 3:6), and I speak to you the word of salvation."

Such was the experience of the Hebrews in the desert of Sinai. Sinai was a lifeless wasteland unrelieved by any green, but the people of today find themselves in another waste place: the teeming confusion of sterile, solitary thoughts that blind the eyes like a sand storm. They thus yearn to rise above such thoughts by means of some sort of "transcendental meditation." They realize that, in order to lead lives worthy of human beings, they must somehow transcend their humanity. But how are they to do that — without mutilating or escaping their humanity, which must be preserved as the treasure it is?

The desire to ascend to heaven is innate in us. But it can take the form symbolized by the tower of Babel, which the Bible (cf. Gen. 11) presents as the sign of unredeemed humanity. For the chosen people, on the other hand, the symbol of ascent is Jacob's ladder. It was on this ladder that Jacob saw the angels coming down from heaven in order to aid a wayfaring humankind that had lost its way (cf. Gen. 28). The angels' descent continues throughout the entire history of salvation, from the Old Testament to the New. Thanks to the Christian faith, we, too, can bring together the antipodes. This faith brings us the good news that the transcendent God became immanent human, that heaven came down to earth, and that the world of ideals took flesh in the concreteness of life — in order to raise up a darkened universe to the light of the Spirit. This is the only solution to the problem that concerns us. Unfortunately, there are many who have not yet grasped this.

Disappointed a thousand times over, people still enthusiastically pursue the tower of Babel. They build it with the bricks of rational ideas and plans they call "spiritual." Even worse off are those who present their banal, sometimes extravagant, feelings as "mystical experiences." And what should we say about those who seek peace by losing themselves in the spirit of the universe, which nirvana-like drowns their personality?

Like the Fathers of the Church, the author of this little book, Marko Rupnik, feels called upon to bear witness to the true Spirit, the Spirit of Christ, who cries, "Abba, Father" (Rom. 8:15) and who speaks to us in the interior burning bush of the heart: "I am here, we meet as two free persons, and yet we are one, just as the Father and the Son are one (John 17:31); your works are yours, but they are also mine; you exist in the material world, the world of human beings, yet you discover to your surprise that by grace you have become spiritual, divine; your 'I' remains within itself, and yet it transcends every human limit."

The present book thus shines like an original pearl in the mire of pseudo-"spiritualities." Without archaism, it explains the main themes of the Christian spiritual tradition to a world absorbed in activity. It thereby retrieves a vision of spirituality that overcomes every form of dualism, moralism, and psychologism and so leads the reader to draw from the riches of the life of the Holy Spirit. In this sense, Rupnik has produced an authentic interpretation of the Second Vatican Council, which set the Church on the path toward recovery of the theological and spiritual paths of the first millennium of the Christian tradition.

Rupnik is an artist known for his paintings and mosaics. Artists know that they don't create new and strange things, but rather are called to reveal what is most real at the very heart of things: the fire that God ignites in them, the fire that does not consume them but enlightens them and gives them life.

Cardinal Tomáš Špidlík, S.J.

The Spiritual Life

AT THE BEGINNING OF THE THIRD Christian millennium we note almost with surprise that people today, regardless of what culture, religion, or geographical area they belong to, demonstrate a great interest in all that is spiritual, in spirituality, and in the spiritual life. It is "surprising" because in the course of the last centuries spirituality and questions of the spiritual life seemed almost to have been put aside.

We want to make a hypothesis here about the motives of this renewed interest. We dwell on the undeniable fact that today the "spiritual question" has returned to the fore. Intellectuals, writers, editorialists, and even art critics and scientists, merchants, and housewives are all concerned about it. Spiritual themes make headlines in magazines and newspapers. Such spirituality grows out of classical references and seeks to establish itself as a common area of interest among those who intend to go beyond the merely phenomenological, beyond the flat explanations of consumerist life. It seeks to establish itself as an area of common understanding for people today who want to go beyond. . . .

However, an infinite number of different concepts of life, of humanity, of God are hidden behind the proposals of "spirituality." These concepts are often quite contradictory among themselves and have no connection to Christianity. They are forms of religiosity that can be called postmodern, indefinable, elusive, which lack an explicit reference to God as Person. They are forms of so-called para-religiosity or of a mixture of beliefs. Many of these forms of spirituality come from the Far East, more or less successfully adapted to the West.

Even among Christians, after the vital inspiration of the Second Vatican Council, the desire was felt to return to the sources to rediscover that force, that inspiration, that "spirit" that was felt to be lacking in a faith life, which had fallen into a rut of cultural projections and mentalities long since passé.

This new vitality assumes diverse expressions according to the environment out of which it grows. Religious orders, for example, can study the history of their founder or foundress in order to refocus on the original impetus of their "spirituality." In daily life it is ever more common to speak of the "spirituality of work," the "spirituality of the family." Every aspect of ordinary life needs to be considered in its spirituality, which is all the more reason to speak of the diverse spirituality of the many vocations: religious, priestly, marital, etc. . . . .

Once upon a time, the word "spirituality" was not so ambiguous. In the past it was possible to clearly define "ascetic" or "spiritual" theology. Today, however, due to the development of a postmodern mentality, these same words can evoke every kind of non-empirical consciousness, from transcendental meditation to yoga, even seances. That is why, more than ever, it is so necessary to avoid ambiguities, to remove extraneous encrustations, and to shed light on the real essence of Christian spirituality.

What is "spiritual"? What is the "spiritual life" in the Christian tradition? I would like to respond to these questions with a synthesis that can constitute a foundation from which to reflect upon the theological and anthropological categories without becoming sidetracked.

This text is for whoever is interested in knowing the Christian sense of spirituality. I hope that these pages will provide a guide from which, with the grace of God, one can begin to live "according to the Spirit."

We are at the beginning of a new era of Christianity. The Church is preparing and embarking upon a new evangelization, a re-evangelization or, better yet, a successive phase of the evangelization of a secularized world. This phase is the latest step in a long process begun in the first centuries of the Christian era. We presently live in a world where Christians are a minority scattered in a diaspora, which is why it is necessary to go deeper, to work on the great themes, on the fundamental points of faith. It is necessary to start over from the essentials in order to help all, even those who are not Christian, to understand the immense spiritual patrimony of the Church and the profundity of her tradition, to draw true spiritual profit from it. We cannot present ourselves to the world drawing attention to the details and nuances that, though important, remain incomprehensible if they lack a setting, a vision of the whole of the organism to which they belong.

I believe this to be the work of the theologian of today: to facilitate the way, to accompany in love with a new, illuminated reflection that desires to enter into the spiritual universe of the Church, assisting the discovery of the essential, concentrating on the basic questions. It is also the job of every Christian, called to be the "light," "salt," "soul" of the world. At the threshold of the third millennium, it is to be hoped that there will be more of those Christians — driven by the love of Christ, foundation of their lives, and by a love for all fellow humans — who will become capable of witnessing to a holy and healthy "spirituality."

Preliminary Clarifications

1. The Spiritual as Non-Material

People . . . are spiritual thanks to their participation in the Spirit, but not thanks to the deprivation and elimination of the flesh.[1]

It was Irenaeus' great contribution to have eliminated the gnostics' concept of the purely spiritual man (in the sense of being "incorporeal").[2]

∽

In speaking, there is often a tendency to understand the spiritual as non-material. In fact, in common parlance, these two realities are often identified with each other.

Such an identification, however, carries a partial, even a deviant, understanding of what is truly spiritual. Understanding the spiritual as non-material means excluding the spiritual dimension of the whole material, physical, and corporeal world. This tendency has found notable acceptance even within the Church. For centuries many preachers exhorted the faithful to occupy themselves with the things of religion (with spiri-

1. Irenaeus, *Adversus haereses*, 5.6.1, in *Contre les hérésies* (Against the Heresies), tr. Adelin Rousseau, SC 153 (Paris: Cerf, 1969).

2. Tomaš Špidlík, *The Spirituality of the Christian East: A Systematic Handbook*, tr. Anthony P. Gythiel (Kalamazoo, MI: Cistercian Publications, 1986), 30. (Translator's note: Where an English translation for a text exists, the pages indicated are always in reference to that version.)

tual things) and, in explaining what they consisted of, preachers encouraged people to be disinterested in the things of this earth, to be uninvolved in material things.

Many examples of such statements come to mind. I recall an episode that shows how pervasive this mentality is as to become common among Christians even in their way of speaking and thinking. At a conference in northern Italy, precisely on the topic of spirituality, I was speaking about the danger of the spiritual becoming identified only with the non-material. A priest, in a protesting manner, said that this tendency was perhaps true in the past but not so today, and that my lecture was too pessimistic. After the conference, a beautiful dinner was offered for the participants. At the end of the evening, we lingered at the table and at a certain moment I heard that same priest saying to another: "How materialistic we are! We have dedicated so little time to spiritual things yet we seem never to have enough for material things!"

2. A Change in Modern Anthropology

[The modern age] brought with it the liberation of humanity's creative forces, spiritual decentralization, and the differentiation of all the spheres of social and cultural life. Science, art, political and economic life, society and culture now become autonomous. . . . The transition from medieval to modern history is synonymous with one from the divine to the human aspects of the world, from the divine depths, interior concentration and the inner core, to an exterior cultural manifestation. This divorce from the spiritual depths, in which humanity's forces had been stored and to which they had been inwardly bound, is accompanied not only by their liberation, but by their passage from the depths to the periphery and the surface of human life, from the medieval religious to secular culture; and it implies the transference of the center of gravity from the divine depths to purely human creation. The spiritual bond with the center of life grows gradually weaker. Modern history therefore conducts Europeans along a path which removes them ever further from the spiritual

center. It is the path of humanity's free experience and the trial of its creative forces.[3]

❧

The difficulty is made greater if, besides the basic ambiguity about what is spiritual, one takes the modern era's cultural change — which is therefore also a change in anthropology — into consideration.

According to an aspect of the anthropology of Saint Paul developed in turn by some of the Church Fathers along the lines of Saint Irenaeus, the whole person is an image of God in body, soul, and spirit. Sin obfuscates this image and impedes the similarity that the salvation of Christ brings to original splendor through baptism. Eastern theology holds that humanity, at its first creation, received the dignity of bearing this image, but its likeness to God must be acquired in cooperation (synergy) with God. Throughout history, one can also note a way of speaking about a person as body and soul, for whom participation in the divine life was explained as supernatural life, as sanctifying grace. The modern era, distrustful of religion's capacity to talk about humanity, instead understands a soul without transcendence, reducing it to the "mind," with no reference to its supernatural dimension. One of the realities that has undergone a great evolution in meaning is the Christian concept of "person."

Historically, this cultural phenomenon is common: After an era of evident "theo-centrism," the rebirth of a period, today called "modernity," begins. It is characterized by a growing anthropocentrism. The epicenter of culture is clearly moved from the divine to the human, from the theological to the philosophical, from the supernatural to the natural sciences. The anthropocentrism of modernity inaugurates a culture of personal autonomy and independence from the religious world. If antiquity's culture was the affirmation of the religious, modernity's is certainly the affirmation of humanity. The cultural and intellectual horizon is moved away from a theological and transcendent horizon to an immanent, an-

3. Nikolai Berdiaev, *Smysl istorii* (Paris: YMCA Press, 1948). Translated into English as *The Meaning of History*, tr. George Reavey (London: G. Bles, 1936), 130-31.

thropological one. Humanity seeks the ultimate criteria of knowledge and its cultural development within the human arena.

As a result, modernity develops a cultural pluralism in a way that is totally autonomous and independent of the Church. The new non-ecclesial culture has completely lost the theological vision of humanity as a unity of body, soul, and spirit. It considers humanity to be more a composite of body and soul, not knowing where and how ultimately to position the presence of spiritual life in it. Modern culture lacks the necessary categories to understand the supernatural in humanity and, when it is taken into consideration, encloses it within the most transcendent sphere imaginable, that of human rationality, which is, in any case, a reality that is completely immanent.

The modern person is therefore seen as just a rational soul and a body. With the progress of modernity, both terms are detached from every reference to the theological and religious dimension that once united the human temporal world to the divine and eternal world.

3. The Mind Is Non-Material

[Often] in fact the term "spiritual" is taken as a synonym . . . of "non-material" within the sphere of the intellect and the natural mind.[4]

Even if they have attempted to recognize a transcendent dimension to reason, enlightenment and positivism have not overcome this reductive vision of humanity. The modern era has completed the process, affirming that humanity is a psychosomatic entity inserted into a social dimension, giving the social a quasi-transcendent dimension. The term "soul" refers to all that is not the body of a person. It acquires an ever more psychologi-

4. Maurizio Costa, *Direzione spirituale e discernimento* (Spiritual Direction and Discernment) (Rome: Edizioni ADP, 1993), 51.

cal meaning until it becomes identified with "mind." Human nature, when it is not a question of medicine, becomes a question of psychology, sociology, politics, and economics.

If the material world corresponds to the world of the body, the non-material world ends up coinciding with that of the mind and, by derivation, with the intellectual world, that of the will and feelings. The spiritual, which is not of the material arena, belongs to the sphere of the mind. According to this way of thinking, the spiritual life is the life of thoughts, of feelings, and of the will.

Even in the Church, Christians submit to the influence of this cultural anthropology according to which the spiritual is understood as non-material and is confused with interiority. The intimate life of the spirit becomes confused with the reality of the mind.

4. *Dangerous Repercussions*

Rationalism is the death of spirituality.[5]

Fasting is good and so are vigils, ascetic practice and xeniteia.[6] *But all these things are but the start, the prelude to the citizenship of*

5. Jacques Maritain, "Descartes and the Cartesian Spirit," in Jacques Maritain, *The Dream of Descartes, Together with Some Essays,* tr. Mabelle L. Andison (New York: Philosophical Library, 1944), 179.

6. This term can be translated as "estranged." It means, like the word *hesychia,* both an inner attitude and an exterior state. It mainly concerns an inner attitude of alienation that has the goal of remaining strangers or pilgrims on the way toward the Celestial City: "we have our citizenship in heaven" (Phil. 3:20). In this sense *xeniteia* is expressed as humility, the rejection of any curiosity or interference in what has nothing to do with oneself, the abandonment of every judgment and evaluation of things in the face of eternity, the uncertainty of the future, and the unpredictable hour of our death. In monastic life, *xeniteia* is expressed in the choice to live in a foreign country and a radical lifestyle on a physical level but also, from the psychological point of view, to live that attitude of alienation from the world. It is an attitude that is given, in an ontological way, to every Christian at the moment of baptism, which makes each a stranger to this world, a person without a homeland, oriented toward the Heavenly City.

heaven, so that it is altogether senseless to put one's trust merely in them.[7]

The principal fruit of prayer is not warmth and sweetness. . . .[8]

∾

The identification of the spiritual with the mind, or with the non-material and ethereal, is in every case a trap. If the spiritual were the intellectual dimension — that is, the sphere of thought and ideas — to become more spiritual would then mean having ever more "elevated" thoughts until one becomes a perfect idealist. In the same way, if the spiritual were the will driven and applied to good thoughts, one would slip into voluntarism. If the spiritual were feelings, one would risk identifying the spiritual with the sentimental.

If they were such, spiritual practices would not be anything other than mental exercises. Prayer would then be identified with mere meditation, understood as a capacity for mental concentration, a mental emptying. The "boom" in ascetic mental practices, of prayer forms that have Eastern and not necessarily religious bases, is one of the fruits of such a misunderstanding. The ambiguity that the attaining of a mythic "spiritual" state proposes, through a constant commitment of the will aided by a technique, often has a utilitarian scope: the conquest of the "good life." It is as if, stressed from the rhythms of modern civilization, people are looking to recoup an interior equilibrium without, however, having to change anything in their own lives. The spiritual life becomes simply a tranquilizer. The more well-being it gives, the better it "works."

There are those who, to measure the consistency and the validity of

7. Symeon Metaphrastis, "Paraphrase of the Homilies of St. Makarios of Egypt," 114, in *Philokalia,* ed. Kallistos Ware, G. E. H. Palmer, and Philip Sherrard (London: Faber & Faber, 1999), 3.335.

8. Theophan the Recluse, "The Fruits of Prayer," in *The Art of Prayer: An Orthodox Anthology,* ed. Hegumen Chariton of Valaam, tr. E. Kadloubovsky and E. M. Palmer (London: Faber & Faber, 1997), 131.

the spiritual life, evaluate the level of difficulty and the ethical ideals that have been achieved. For them, the more "demanding" means the more spiritual.

5. *Sacramental Crisis*

> *It is not enough to contemplate God, humanity must be divinized by its contemplation: The new religion cannot be simply a passive reverence for God* (theosebeia) *or an act of worship* (theolatreia) *but must be activity in and with him* (theourgia), *a common movement of God and humans to transform natural humanity into a spiritual race, a divine people; it is not a matter of creation out of nothing but of transformation, a transubstantiation of matter into spirit, of the life of this world into the life of God.*[9]

~

This ambiguous vision of spirituality, which can in a certain way be called "gnostic," can extend into entire spheres of faith. Let us take the sacraments as an example. In confession a person confesses a sin linked in some way to a minor psychological disorder. The person receives absolution, recites some Hail Marys as a penance, but the problem does not go away. Although continuing to confess time after time, the person becomes more and more discouraged. It can happen that the person finally stops going to confession, thinking that it had not helped at all. Confessing did not help the person not to commit "that" sin anymore.

This person had wanted to experience freedom from an obsession, however big or small, to savor the fruits of a truly spiritual life. If this per-

---

9. Vladimir Solov'ëv, *Duchovnja osnovy žizni,* in *Sobranie Sočinenii,* vol. 3 (Brussels: Foyer Oriental Chrétien, 1966). Translated into English as *God, Man, and the Church: The Spiritual Foundations of Life,* tr. Donald Attwater (Milwaukee, WI: Bruce Publishing Co., 1938), 131.

son could not succeed, it is because the person's spiritual life, locked within a mental or ethical trap, had become ineffective.

It may happen that this same person gets better and is healed by going to a psychotherapist or a psychologist. The expert who studies the conscious and subconscious world and the relationship between its rational and instinctive-passionate aspects must have been able to do something where the confessor failed. It is a phenomenological observation: More and more the psychologist is substituted for the confessor to the point that many priests orient themselves toward psychology and end up being more psychologists than priests.

At the basis of this new phenomenon there is the usual flawed vision of the spiritual life. The confessor who reduces the spiritual life to the world of the mind — ignoring the spiritual and therefore liberating vigor of the Spirit — becomes a confessor who is powerless, incapable of offering a taste of the transforming power of Love in daily life. If the confessor's vision of the person and of spiritual life does not see the Holy Spirit as the One who inhabits humanity, confession becomes problematic. The real protagonist of confession is actually the Holy Spirit; not taking him into account directs the very sacramental practice down a blind alley.

Let us also take the Eucharist as an example. If the spiritual is the non-material, how can the physical realities of the bread and wine as perfectly spiritual Eucharistic realities be explained? If the spiritual is identified with the non-material, there is no way of explaining to the faithful the transubstantiation that occurs in the Eucharist. This mystery is spoken of with embarrassment, at times clutching at straws. A murky, approximating terminology cannot be avoided. It almost seems that the current mentality makes it difficult to conceive of how cosmic material and human labor can become authentically spiritual, in the truest sense of the word, in the Eucharist. This "cultural embarrassment" in presenting the mystery of the Eucharist has contributed to a slow emptying of the unequaled sacrament of the "taste" of God. Without the "taste," without knowledge of him and his salvation, the Eucharist becomes an arid rite, a far-away mystery that does not touch the hearts of people or reach into their lives.

In the end it becomes just the pretext for Sunday Mass. Even there, with the affirmation of the freedom of the individual and the "demythologizing" of ecclesiastical authority, people have stopped feeling obligated to fulfill the precept. Some have continued by force of habit, others have substituted what in their eyes is nothing other than a traditional practice with one of the many modern Sunday activities that cultural pluralism offers.

6. The Question of Nature and the Spiritual

"Person" signifies the irreducibility of a human to nature. . . . [Human beings] do not exist in themselves beyond the nature which they "enhypostatize" and which they constantly exceed.[10]

∽

In speaking of humanity, our tradition has developed the concept of nature more than that of person. Neither positive nor negative in itself, it is a given fact, due to the evolution of theological reflection on one of the dimensions of the wealth of faith. This tendency has permitted the exposition of many new possibilities in researching humanity. It has increased the splendor of our tradition, but it also carries some risks.

Every theological conquest needs a second phase of thinking to integrate the trains of thought that it has momentarily abandoned in its development. Any specific analytic deepening whatsoever requires a confrontation in order to be integrated with other options that have been omitted. This has also occurred in anthropology in reference to the question of nature/person. Today, we better understand that which refers to the agapic principle in a person (love as a person's source and foundation).

Nature, considered as that which is common to all persons, as a kind of universal form, becomes a reality that can be studied, a reality with its laws that, once known, render it "controllable." On the basis of this con-

---

10. Vladimir Lossky, *In the Image and Likeness of God,* tr. John H. Erickson and Thomas E. Bird (Crestwood, NY: St. Vladimir's Seminary Press, 1985), 120.

cept of nature a strong, scientific rationality is developed which brings science almost to an identification with technology, that is, with knowing how to "govern" material realities and knowing how to exploit to the maximum the potentiality of both cosmic and human nature. According to such a concept of nature, a person is nothing other than an individual, that is, a particular form of the universal human nature. The perfection of nature resides in its own law; the perfection of the individual therefore will consist of conformity to this law of human nature.

A similar vision has led to an understanding of the spiritual and the spiritual life as a perfection of life. It is as if even the spiritual world, having its own nature, had its own laws to which human nature, in itself not yet spiritual or in any case fallen, must conform.

It is as if at a certain moment we were to find ourselves before a human nature and a spiritual nature with their own laws. However, before the affirmation of humanity in its self-determination, something affirmed from the start of the modern era, there is a step missing in concluding that the spiritual life is "non-material," even "against nature." Thus, spiritual exercises limit and impoverish human nature, making it into something else. The renunciations and the asceticism that the spiritual life foresees are presented as something like a violence against nature.

If instead humanity gives preference to the spiritual nature, there is the risk of finding ourselves before a rationalistic-ethical interpretation of the spiritual life reduced to its own rules. From this point the spiritual life slides into a mere ethics and is understood more and more as morality. If the spiritual life is identified with the ethical-moral life, the ways of the spiritual life automatically become the ways of moral asceticism.

Human nature is, however, understood only in light of the agapic principle that personalizes it and from which the real meaning of spiritual life is disclosed. It is a meaning that embraces even the dimension of objectivity constituted by human nature in relationship and in love. Human nature belongs to the person and is that by which the spiritual life, the whole person, is personalized.

7. The Concept of Nature, the Sciences, and the Spiritual Life

The theologian must participate in prayer and in the whole life of the Church because theology has knowing God and making him known as its goal. But one cannot know God if one does not enter into a personal relationship of love with him and with believers through prayer and service.[11]

The recent evolution of theology has made the need for other genres more keenly felt. In these days its procedures have led the theologian to seek secondary disciplines. . . . Their contribution is useful, if not indispensable. But in their research and teaching they have ended up taking the greater, if not the whole, space. In this case, theology is eliminated. . . . Properly speaking, theology requires faith, while these secondary disciplines do not presuppose it. . . . Without faith there is no theology. . . . In each age, theology is influenced by the conceptions of study in the diverse areas of human knowledge. Thus, after three or four centuries it submits to the repercussions of research and the experimental sciences.[12]

∽

The dialectic tension between spirituality and science, a situation fostered by a particular historic development, is also situated against the backdrop of the scenario that sees the concept of nature as predominant, and therefore encourages the development of scientific areas of study. If in the first millennium theology was born in the environment of the monasteries, in the late Middle Ages and in the modern era it has found its milieu in the universities. Even the spiritual life, an integral part of theology, has undergone the effects of the same development.

11. Dumitru Staniloaë, *La genie de l'Orthodoxie* (The Spirit of Orthodoxy), tr. Dan Ilie Ciobotea (Paris: Desclée de Brouwer, 1985), 135.

12. Michel Dupuy, "La notion de spiritualité" (The Notion of Spirituality), in *Dictionnaire de spiritualité* (Paris: Beauchesne, 1990), 14.1166-1167.

Theology was linked to its "handmaid," philosophy. Together with philosophy, theology reflected the effects of the evolution of modern thought, above all in the questions that regarded epistemology and, later, the empirical sciences. This influence affected theology to the point of its having to present itself as a science, in the modern sense, in order to maintain the possibility of dialog with the dominant way of thinking. This relationship between modernity and science has cost theology a great price. It has become separated from faith and from the ecclesial life. When theology became a discipline of study like the others, when it became possible to be a theologian simply by studying theology at the university, then the mutual and essential connection between theology and faith, in which theology was useful as a nourishment to personal faith and to that of the community, ended. Being a theologian no longer meant an essential participation in the life of the Church, least of all in the liturgical community, which is active in prayer and fraternal charity.

When this phenomenon became more widespread, theology found itself forced into opening a new field of study, that of spirituality, founding chairs of spiritual theology, and then institutes or faculties of spirituality. Thus the schism between theology and the spiritual life was definitively sanctioned, a paradigm of the even greater schism already beginning to form between theology and life, between theology and faith.

This division reflected the evolution of theological thought on nature. As the understanding of nature became more an object of study of the modern sciences, the more the space between the spiritual and the spiritual life diminished. The modern imperative of the necessity of rational clarity with regard to the subject, the object, and the world entered into theology. It blurred the essentiality of the personal agapic principle and as a result the essentiality of the spiritual life, or else it limited it to specific areas of life.

8. A Temptation toward Monism, Pantheism, or Dualism

In the Christian understanding of the relation existing between God and the world, it is first necessary to exclude two polar opposites: pantheistic, or atheistic, monism on the one hand and the dualistic conception of creation on the other. According to the monistic doctrine, the world is self-sufficient and can be understood from itself. . . . At the opposite pole to cosmism or cosmotheism is dualism. Dualism is characterized by the recognition of the createdness of the world. However, for dualism the world is created not by one creator but by two. . . . It is easy to see the religious absurdity of such a dualism, which is only a masked form of atheism. . . .[13]

⌇

Another possible misunderstanding of the spiritual has to do with pantheism and monism, recurring temptations in the history of Christianity. Understanding the spiritual as separated from life, from the material and historic world, raises suspicions that there is a way to understand the world dualistically. If the material and the spiritual are opposed, perfection will come with the elimination of one of the two (monism) or in making all things equally important (pantheism).

Monistic tendencies and currents explain reality as One, the perfection of which absorbs multiplicity. The One can be the spiritual, for which the world, in its most elevated aspect, cancels out its multiple materiality in order to merge itself in the spiritual. Tendencies that prefer the pantheistic formula instead consider that every thing, even the slightest, is part of the spiritual world.

However, as the great thinkers of the past have indicated, the mental structures of monism and pantheism are essentially the same. Typical of an atheistic vision of the world, they are inherently materialistic structures. The structure proper to faith, however, is the reciprocal recognition of two subjects: a dialogue. If in monism the other is destined to disappear, in pantheism the other is not recognized in its religious dimension in that there is no recognition of the other as Absolute, a recognition that does characterize a faith relationship. In order to compensate for this fundamental emptiness, a pantheistic vision of the world can produce an

13. Sergius Bulgakov, *Nevesta Agnca* (Paris: YMCA Press, 1945). Translated into English as *The Bride of the Lamb*, tr. Boris Jakim (Grand Rapids, MI: Eerdmans, 2002), 3, 4, 5.

elaborate and rich mysticism, but without the transcendent God and without there being a true religious principle. Monism and pantheism are visions of the world in which mysticism is simply used as an element that feigns being a religious principle, but in reality never flows into the religious, that is, into openness toward the other.

9. Material and Spiritual Dualism and the Consequences of Separating Body and Spirit

To assert that God does not "interest himself" in our material wants is to justify atheism by putting limits to the Godhead.[14]

When, as happens with pantheism, there is no real relational opening towards the other and an ambiguous mysticism disguises the fatalism within refined materialistic tendencies, the human spirit becomes enslaved in the world and in historical processes. Such mysticism then is only an attempt to soften the determinism at the core of such a vision.

Equally atheistic is every dualistic vision that excludes God from the material and corporeal world. The concept of a God who is not interested in history expresses a vision of life, of the spiritual, and of religion that is radically opposed to the Christian faith, that is contrary to principal Christological dogmas. Behind beautiful spiritual and devotional labels (innocent attitudes, disinterest in the world and in history, etc.) is hidden a powerful weapon at the disposal of anyone who has an interest in acting against Christian faith and life.

History itself confirms that a spirituality that separates body from spirit, confined to the immaterial seeking to lead humanity to a disinterest in the world, is against charity. It is a sin of deficiency and carries out an injustice. Whenever a part is taken from the whole, if one part is domi-

14. Vladimir Solov'ëv, *God, Man, and the Church: The Spiritual Foundations of Life*, 44.

nant over all, an injustice is always committed. A religious vision in which God is excluded from the material and corporeal world can also give rise to injustice. This is as if to say: This is the world and God does not enter into it.

If an injustice finds justification and strength in a religion, this historically has meant justification of a revolutionary solution to overthrow, together with the injustice, the religion that permits it.

Something also should be said about the materialism that is at the heart of a vision of the human body so easily identified with matter. The body is not matter that is opposed to the spirit. Saint Paul speaks of the spiritual body, and many modern authors (for example, Sergius Bulgakov) have offered splendid meditations on the spiritual dimension of the body as the foundation for faith in the resurrection. Identifying the body with matter makes it difficult to understand the great dogmas of Christianity, therefore making theology and the spirituality of the Incarnation, the Transfiguration, and obviously the Resurrection incomprehensible.

10. Feeling "All Right"

Vainglory is a change of nature, a perversion of character, a taking note of criticism. As for its quality, it is a waste of work and sweat, a betrayal of treasure, an offspring of unbelief, a harbinger of pride, a shipwreck in port. . . . A vainglorious person is a believer — and an idolator. Apparently honoring God, he or she is actually out to please not God but humans.[15]

Some say that the lack of oil in the lamps of the foolish virgins means a lack of good deeds in their lifetime. Such an interpretation is not quite correct. Why should they be lacking in good deeds if they are called virgins, even though foolish ones? . . . I, the humble one, think that what they were lacking was the grace of the All-Holy Spirit of

---

15. John Climacus, *The Ladder of Divine Ascent,* tr. Colm Luibheid and Norman Russell (Mahwah, NJ: Paulist Press, 1982), 201-202.

*God. These virgins practiced the virtues, but in their spiritual igno-
rance, they supposed that the Christian life consisted merely in doing
good works.*[16]

A spirituality that is dualistic at heart, that is gnostically organized, can
inflate people to the extent that they feel "all right," perfect. If the spiritual life is understood as an intellectual activity, then it is sufficient to ad-
here to determined doctrinal presuppositions, to observe certain principles, to follow a determined logic, to engage in precise practices in order
to be "spiritual." Such a "spirituality" runs the risk of not permitting any
communion on the social or ecclesial level. Models of behavior tied to re-
stricted groups are created, against which persons end up measuring
themselves and their spiritual lives. It is as if to say that those who fit such
models can feel themselves "all right" and can therefore easily judge those
who do not live or succeed in living according to the same style. Thus a
"classification" of persons based on whether they belong to that model or
not is developed. Spirituality is then exchanged for a conformity to the
rules.

Conformity means that if in a seminary there is a rector who places
great importance on visits to the Blessed Sacrament and he is seen passing
in front of the chapel reciting his breviary, a seminarian can be tempted to
enter the chapel simply to please his superior. Is that visit to the Blessed
Sacrament a spiritual one? Does it not have more to do with opportunism
and hypocrisy, and therefore only with the psychological world of that
seminarian?

By this I mean to say that a partial comprehension of spirituality, a
spirituality "in parts," ends up leading to psychological deformities. By itself it weighs on the character of the person, posing moral problems. Understanding spirituality in a gnostic way, valuing only the intellectual
sphere, easily leads to a deviation that could be called "making the partic-

16. Seraphim of Sarov, *Spiritual Instructions*, vol. 1 of *Little Russian Philokalia*
(Ouzinkie, AK: St. Herman Press, 1991), 88.

ular absolute." This means that those who confuse the "spiritual" with the high ideas they have of life, with the beautiful thoughts that perhaps come to them during prayer, believe that they will be all the more spiritual if they try to be mentally more attentive to God and dedicate more time to the things they consider to be spiritual.

According to this criterion, one arrives at the absurd affirmation that spiritual being depends on the time dedicated to spiritual practices. Does this not perhaps bring one to favor a schism between prayer and lived experience, between prayer and daily behavior? Life today is not structured along the lines of prayer but those of work. Is the era of "spiritual persons" over?

11. The Pendulum Reaction

A long series of philosophical doctrines, each of which asserted itself as the absolute truth . . . was then refuted by the following doctrine as error.[17]

A dualistic positing of the spiritual life produces, as we have said, moralism, voluntarism, legalism, and other similar nuisances. Sooner or later, a reaction is born in this context. If the entire spiritual life is concentrated in the world that, according to this mindset, is the world of the soul, but is considered, as I have shown, only the psychological world, one soon arrives at an unsupportable tension. With thought and will (called "soul") one attempts to direct, contain, and control all corporeal reality: instincts, passions, desires, or needs. The tension becomes ever stronger, almost unbearable. However they try, people feel that they cannot stand it for long and that, sooner or later, this entire reality will explode. In the meantime,

17. Vladimir Solov'ëv, *Krizis zapadnoj filosofi,* in *Sobranie Sočinenii,* vol. 1 (Brussels: Foyer Oriental Chrétien, 1966). Translated into English as *The Crisis of Western Philosophy: Against the Positivists,* tr. Boris Jakim (Hudson, NY: Lindisfarne Press, 1996), 34.

the spiritual life, understood as the practice of prayer, becomes a purely immanent exercise, flavorless asceticism, incapable of offering a true liberation to people held prisoner between the intellect and the passions. To alleviate the pressure they may start to sink to quantitative compromises, letting themselves go as far as conceivably possible. Sometimes people can even slide into actual pathologies, where this rigorous attitude — gnostic in any case, and not really religious — triggers a subconscious tension previously latent, transforming it into a neurosis.

In some the passionate part rebels so violently that, in order to maintain a balance, they find it necessary to build a "false philosophy," to rationalize their vices and instincts. It is a sort of "defense," a well-thought-out justification sustained by many philosophical, psychological, cultural, and even spiritual arguments. To disguise their concessions they begin to cite Sacred Scripture. The Fathers already saw this as one of the most serious spiritual aberrations. Nevertheless, this phenomenon is one of the most frequent. People, in order to prove their uniqueness from one another, to demonstrate their diversity, wrap their ideas in biblical quotations and in sacred teachings. However, this does nothing other than affirm their own will with a stubborn selfishness.

The dualism that opposes idea-matter, intellect-passions, will-instincts also explains the long series of oscillations that has occurred in the course of the history of human thought. In philosophy, since the era of Greek classicism, as a reaction to a great idealist, a great materialist always follows. Feuerbach and Marx come after Hegel. In art, the baroque follows the idealist renaissance, expressionism comes after impressionism, and so on.

The same reactions also occur in the theological and ecclesial fields. In a religious order, where previously study and intellectual work was emphasized, a reaction made up of pure praxis, of direct commitment, almost "rejection" of the study that had been sought after in the past, is found today.

Even in the history of peoples and cultural traditions, where an ascetic, rigorous, legalistic Catholicism was most prevalent, after a brief period of explosion and liberation from the yoke, there follow decades of rebellion against any authority and a break with every link to the past. The same happened in Protestant countries. Once the stronghold of the puritanical and moralistic conception of faith, they are now subject to the most ruthless liberalism and ethical subjectivism.

12. A Psychological Reaction

It does not seem to me that psychology must be acknowledged as an integrative function of the human person . . . rather, it is respect for the mystery of the human person that demands it.[18]

∾

The most common reaction that comes from a gnostic understanding of spirituality has been, in my opinion, the psychological one. After a period of the hard line of the spiritual life reduced to the mind, in which people often wind up doing violence to themselves, a soft line arises, that of psychology. A spirituality of "feeling" responds to an abstract and conceptual spirituality that divorces the body from the spirit. What counts is only "how it feels." After an imposed spiritual direction the reaction is toward psychological counseling, simply listening, in which it is better not to say anything, nor to intervene.

In gnostic spirituality, psychological reality was undervalued or ignored. It was set up toward strong colors without much nuance. A spiritual life was the fruit of the will, of constant exercise, and of asceticism that sufficed to overcome difficulties and temptations. If this was a fundamentalist position, today the other extreme rules. It almost seems that the spiritual life is impossible without taking the subconscious and psychological history of the individual into account. Psychologizing, in reality, is merely the other face of the same spiritual gnosticism. It is difficult to affirm, however, that a positive step forward in spirituality has been taken while it is still locked within the ego.

It is important that the spiritual life today not fall into the trap of automatism, a reaction that is actually the same as that concept of spiritual-

18. Costa, *Direzione spirituale e discernimento*, 96.

ity being refuted. In gnostic-legalist concepts it was difficult to construct a life with a profound dimension of faith. As a reaction to this, by responding with psychology, the mechanism of the "pendulum" is triggered again. The healthy and positive step would instead be that of an openness of the self to a personal God, to the transcendent, an openness that orients us to neighbor and, at the same time, to all of creation. Psychology does not actually overcome the gnostic deception, nor is it a substantial novelty. It is only a formal retouching of gnosticism and as such often does not succeed in helping people transcend their own worlds but rather keeps them locked within their problems.

In books on spirituality, which fill the shelves of bookstores today, many texts written by priest-psychologists can be found. It is rare, however to find one that speaks of a real opening to a transcendence that incorporates everything, every aspect of life. It seems that the spiritual terminology of "relationship," of "personal dimension," of "the God who has a face" is almost unknown. Psychology has penetrated the spiritual life and the manuals of spirituality, once again upsetting the fundamental sense of the "spiritual."

In the years of great enthusiasm for psychology, many novice masters were chosen primarily on the basis of their competence in psychology. At first it seemed that, in spite of the diversity of religious orders and their situations in various geographical and cultural areas, this work on their psychological dimension had been of use to the novices. They left the novitiate with a more serene psyche, as if "cleansed" and reorganized. Some years later, there appeared the first difficulties, precisely in the area of what the founders of religious institutes and the charisms of these institutes considered authentic "spiritual life."

The aspect that psychological approaches had undervalued and did not deal with made itself felt. These novices had probably learned to know themselves better, but they had not been initiated into a daily life with Christ or into the spiritual dimension of apostolic life and the life of study. Formation was primarily focused on therapeutic work, which was given priority. If this had a good outcome, the candidate would be promoted in the novitiate.

The suspicion therefore is that, under the standard of psychology, the dualistic trap of gnosticism is hidden once again. Rather, it is a new dualism with a "first" and a "then." First one does therapy and then one can be spiritual. Is it true that a therapeutic process is the condition for a spiritual journey? In any case, the real danger of falling into the logic of an "either-or" exists. We must choose either psychology or spirituality, either "feeling good" or "moralism." On a purely psychological level, inasmuch as the "psychological" and the "spiritual" dimensions are distinct, it is practically impossible to reach any real integration. Instead, we make compromises which do nothing other than confirm that one dimension cannot be reduced to the other.

If psychology and spirituality are not well distinguished from one another, we simply create a confusion that does not help heal the difficulties made evident through therapy. A therapeutic treatment can bring one to the understanding of a problem with a psychological origin but, that being said, the person may not be in a position to resolve it. The realities we become conscious of through therapy are therefore cured. This does not mean that they become a spiritual reality, or that through them the true personal God is encountered. These realities take place through Christ in order that, at the end of time, they might be found transfigured, having become an integral part of the whole person. This is the true integration that occurs, however, only within the sphere of faith, the sphere of personal relationship. Thus, it is necessary to look for the way in which psychology and the spiritual life are not in conflict or confused with one another, but rather exist harmoniously.

13. Disintegration

Christ "is not different from the virtues that fill him." He is at the same time Justice, Wisdom, and Truth.[19]

Seek to acquire the perfect virtue, adorned with all that pleases God. It is called a single virtue, because it encompasses in itself the beauty

19. Špidlík, *The Spirituality of the Christian East,* 291.

and variety of all the virtues. As a royal diadem can never be set only with pearls, without other precious stones, so the single virtue cannot exist without the beauty of the various virtues.[20]

~

A vision in which the spiritual life is entrapped within the human mind produces a fracture in the so-called spiritual person, even in that which is traditionally called virtue. People who follow their spiritual ideals can also achieve a valuable perfection, but if there is some disunity in their basic behavior, they must suppose that that perfection is the fruit of a spiritual gnosticism rather than of the Spirit. For example, a person can be well experienced in what is identified, at a formal level, with poverty. The same person can, however, judge a neighbor harshly and speak ill of others. Perhaps such people do not realize it or, if they are able to "see themselves," they might try to fix their contradictoriness with a pedagogical-ethical rationalization, with a sort of "program" for conquering even the virtue of charity. The spiritual life thus becomes a military campaign made up of virtuous positions to be conquered, and it loses the essence of a complete, living organism at one with the person. Maybe only after years of hard work and almost useless tension, that person understands that he or she has been on the wrong road.

Spiritual gnosticism of whatever type, whether psychological or moralistic, is recognized precisely in the incapacity to see the connections between the various dimensions of the person and the various facts of life. The spiritual life embraces thoughts, emotions, and physicality. There is no event in daily life, however insignificant, that is excluded, untouched by the life of the spirit.

A gnosticism with psychological tendencies is easily recognized because people "affected" by it, finding themselves faced with an authentically lived spiritual life, lack the precise epistemological tools to know and judge such a life. It is because of a psychological gnosticism that the deeds of some holy lives are judged as having nothing to say to the world and, at

20. Evagrius, *Sermo asceticus* (Ascetic Sermon), ed. Rome, 1.61.

best, should only be shown as "episodes" in the showcase of history. Those who judge lack the relational dimension of love as a sphere in which to understand gestures, mentality, and spiritual practices. It happens, therefore, that even the most loving gesture, driven by an intimate knowledge of the word of God and truly undertaken as a free act, comes to be judged by psychological gnosticism as a violence to oneself, as a religious fanaticism, etc.

Spiritual gnosticism is as if blind to a truly spiritual life. It is unable to recognize it, having only considered it mentally without entering into a truly religious dimension. Its "spiritual" life is governed by an internal philosophical, psychological, or legalistic logic, which is the very problem — it is governed by logic. When face to face with a spiritually authentic event, it frames it in a conceptual structure of religiosity, that is, in psychological, legalistic, or moral terms, labeling it as spiritualism, fundamentalism, or integralism, because these are the categories of its way of thinking. This attitude becomes even more explicit when dealing with "spiritual fatherhood" or spiritual direction. For a psychological type of spiritual gnosticism, a letter of Saint Ignatius is an imposition, a saying of a desert Father even worse, counsel from a spiritual father to pray better is paternalism, an attack on personal liberty, a restriction.

Any type of gnosticism always has to do with a disintegration. For example, gnostics can be completely absorbed in a great battle, even an evangelical one, like justice or equality. Realizing such a great ideal can completely absorb them. It can also make them unfair, bullying, overbearing with whoever does not see things the same way, with those who thus become estranged, even adversarial.

It is a phenomenon observable even within the life of the Church. It is possible to "fight" for one group while at the same time wounding another. Those who raise the flag of high spiritual standards at times end up causing much suffering to their own community. Defending or affirming prayer in a community can cause many negative, critical, disparaging, uncomprehending judgments to fall upon its members. Affirming prayer can paradoxically affirm violence.

Another source of profound disintegration arises in the Spirit through the relationship with the world. It happens that even in the spiritual life today we are confronted with the world before knowing the contents of faith. We end up adopting the criteria, norms, or values that are dominant in the world, transplanting them directly into the life of faith, without purifying them so that they might be integrated into an organic whole. Therefore, these elements remain like islands apart, almost foreign bodies that, instead of orienting one towards God, slowly become the point of reference for orientation toward the world. Thus the dualistic gap between the divine and the human, between the spiritual and the pastoral, between being with God and being with those people who need us is widened. The person, divided between two opposing directions, falls into an internal contradiction that causes suffering and unbearable confusion.

There are many important realities in the world that do not necessarily have a spiritual meaning and which must still pass through a way of spiritualization. For the beginner walking the spiritual path who still is not radically oriented to Christ, distinguishing what is and is not spiritual in the midst of the supermarket of the world can be very difficult. Macarius the Great says that the soul of the one who insists on following two opposing principles sooner or later dies to the spiritual life.

The remedy is certainly a balanced teaching, without closures or radical extremes that create confusion and cause the loss of one's identity. The privileged route is, however, that of the process of hypostatization of one's own culture. This means the maturation of values and cultural realities only in the direction that favors a culture of the heart, that is, a culture of interpersonal communication. The hypostatization of culture means that the entire culture receives the mark of relationship and rapport, which thus becomes the sphere of communication. That which is at the service of communication is a true culture, a living culture, because within it people encounter one another. It is precisely this encounter and communication that make of culture a living memory. Remembering the other and what he or she has communicated, or in remembering the encounter, we see again that we find ourselves in the realm of the spiritual. The spiritual person is a person of communication and of an always-greater love. Human values are transfigured, not annihilated; the realities of the world, assumed into Christ, become spiritualized. The things and the values of the world die in whatever does not permit them to truly be "at the service" of communication, of interpersonal encounter.

14. The Spiritual Belongs to the Person

One insists principally on the fact that every life comes from God and that the "Spirit" was breathed onto the face of humanity at the beginning of creation. Human beings cannot develop their own "spirituality" except in relation to God. Every diminishment of this relationship is, therefore, an attack on the life of the person.[21]

∽

If the spiritual were not inseparably linked to the Divine Persons, the spiritual life could not be inseparably linked to human persons. If my spiritual reality is impersonal, separated from the divine Person of Christ, the temptation will always exist to choose a title, to find a label, and to affirm it as the whole while overlooking the personality that is each person's. This leads to an idealization, to an abstract approach that sooner or later is revealed as deviant and provokes illness because it fails to take the living person into consideration.

Forcing a person into boxes and formulas of spirituality is not spiritual. It is only with difficulty that whatever is not truly founded in a living reality could help someone toward a better, more authentic life. If I want to show someone the spiritual life and help him or her to attain it, the first spiritual act on my part consists in considering the concrete person being addressed in whom I seek what is spiritual in order to make it come alive. The spiritual life is life precisely because it touches upon the living Person. Separating the spiritual from the theologically and anthropologically meaningful realities of the Person means opening the door to gnosticism, fideism, magic, and to many other "-isms" of that type.

21. Tomaš Špidlík and Innocenzo Gargano, *La spiritualità dei Padri greci ed orientali* (The Spirituality of the Greek and Eastern Fathers) (Rome: Borla, 1983), 8.

Spirituality is not a field unto itself. It is an integral part of true dogma. Separated from theology and from theological anthropology — which are like two pillars rising from the same base — spirituality becomes something other than what it is in Christianity, something unable to respond to what it truly is. Whatever is not joined to life, is not rooted in it, cannot serve life. Further, it makes individuals deviate from and can fatally distance them from concrete daily life.

The Nature of the Spiritual and the Spiritual Life

15. The Spiritual in the Icon

Historical development is a long and difficult process from the zoo-human to the theo-human state.[22]

The perfect human being succeeds in uniting all the elements of the person: Each of them is penetrated by the force of the Holy Spirit.[23]

The more love increases in you, the more beauty increases; for love itself is the soul's beauty.[24]

Father Seraphim took me very firmly by the shoulders and said: "We are both in the Spirit of God now, my dear. Why don't you look at me?" I replied, "I cannot look, Father, because your eyes are flashing like lightning. Your face has become brighter than the sun. . . ." Father Seraphim said, "Don't be alarmed, your Godliness! Now you

22. Vladimir Solov'ëv, *Opravdanie dobra*, in *Sobranie Sočinenii*, vol. 8 (Brussels: Foyer Oriental Chrétien, 1966), 174. Translated into English as *The Justification of the Good: An Essay on Moral Philosophy*, tr. Nathalie A. Duddington (London: Constable, 1918), cf. 246-247.

23. Tomaš Špidlík, *Manuale fondamentale di spiritualità* (Basic Handbook of Spirituality) (Casale Monferrato: Piemme, 1993), 13.

24. Augustine, *Tractates on the First Epistle of John*, 9.9, tr. John W. Rettig (Washington, DC: CUA Press, 1995), 258.

yourself have become as bright as I am. You are now in the fullness of the Spirit of God yourself; otherwise you would not be able to see me. . . ."[25]

❧

In the Christian tradition we can find an authentic meaning of the spiritual in the icon of the Face of Christ called *Acheiropoietos* ("not made by human hands").

The portraits of Christ in icons, and likewise all the portraits of the saints, are designed on a composition of four concentric circles. Within this structure of four circles, beginning from the innermost one, the profound meaning of the spiritual is concealed.

The first circle is found on the forehead, between the eyes, and is generally invisible. It is the circle of the Holy Spirit's participation, that is, the capacity given by the Creator to humanity to open itself to and to welcome the personal participation of the Holy Spirit. It is the life-giving point because it is the indwelling of the Lord himself, the giver of life.

The second circle includes the forehead and the eyes. It is the circle of the soul, that is, of the world of the mind, of intelligence, of feeling, and of the will.

The third circle embraces the hair, the mouth, and the beard and represents the body, that is, the most exposed dimension in humanity. The hair whitens and falls. The mouth is the most sensual part because it indicates the need to eat in order to survive. This circle therefore expresses the remembrance of physical vulnerability and of the mortality of the human body.

The fourth circle represents the icon's circle of purest gold, of the most golden and brilliant yellow. Commonly called the halo, it is the light of the Holy Spirit that, from the innermost circle, penetrates the whole mental and corporeal world and envelops the person in such brightness that it becomes perceptible to others.

25. Seraphim of Sarov, *Spiritual Instructions,* 110-111.

The Holy Spirit, this Revealer of God, this mysterious cloud that descended when God descended among his people, this Shadow of the Most High that communicates God making him flesh in the Virgin, this Holy Spirit completes the work of sanctification, orienting everything toward the Son and crying out "Abba," giving to all in Christ the imprint of filiation, so that he might deliver all to the Father.

This Holy Spirit who communicates the entire truth reminds us of the wonders of God and makes us recognize the work of salvation. The Holy Spirit who, as at Pentecost, gives human eyes the capacity to see the Face of God in the Crucified, makes us see how each person ought to be, haloed by light. If humanity so desires, the Holy Spirit brings the fruits of divine life into history, into the new humanity. The fruit of the Spirit, in the forms listed by Saint Paul in the Letter to the Galatians, leads back to the hymns of charity and makes humanity similar, in its lived experience, to God.

The icon shows us where the Holy Spirit resides in a person and how this indwelling is seen. Only when the Holy Spirit penetrates the intellectual and mental world, only when the Spirit moves the gestures and actions of the body, penetrating the entirety of the person, only then does he become visible to all. The person who allows the self to be progressively filled with the Holy Spirit makes the actions of the Spirit apparent, reminds others of God, recalls others to God, becomes a communicator of, a narration of God. The dwelling place of the Spirit in humanity is the whole person, and this sacred presence is perceived through the action of the Holy Spirit himself. A person filled with the light and the fruits of the Holy Spirit becomes a living compass pointing towards God. That person becomes an image, a likeness of God. That person becomes a word of God that others can see and touch.

The *Acheiropoietos* icon suggests the true meaning of the spiritual in the Christian tradition. It is an action of the Holy Spirit that extends to the whole universe and reminds things, events, and persons of God, speaking to us of him, narrating his wonders and the history of salvation, orienting us toward him, communicating him until finally we are reunited with him.

If this is the effect of the spiritual, no one can be called "spiritual." It is others who are able to recognize a spiritual person as a word of God. It is others who show, in transforming themselves, that this person has recalled God to them and has brought them back to him. It is others who recognize the action of charity that allows them to feel the love of God in their lives. It is others who recognize a spiritual mentality in a person that reminds them of the gospel and its mentality. The spiritual person incarnates a mentality similar to that of Christ.

That is why the spiritual cannot be identified with only the mental, ethereal, or immaterial world. All of humanity, the entire physical and historical cosmic world, is called to become spiritual. The cosmic, corporeal, material, and physical are called just as the rest, otherwise dualism would be inevitable and salvation would never be achieved. After original sin, it is precisely the body with its inclinations that most rebels against becoming spiritual and that tries to escape the true meaning of that word. It should also not be forgotten that at times the body can place itself at the service of love while it is the mentality, often stubborn and very clever in taking care of its own business and avoiding letting itself be permeated by love, that can be insensible.

16. The Spiritual Life

Incorporeal spirits will never be spiritual persons. It is our substance, that is, the union of the soul and the flesh, receiving the Spirit of God, that constitutes the spiritual person.[26]

The spiritual life is life in and with the Holy Spirit.[27]

This assures that the I, after a more complete turn inward, discovers in itself something still more intimate than its own intimacy. It knows and recognizes this in its impotence and devotion as some-

---

26. Irenaeus, *Adversus haereses*, 5.8.2.
27. Špidlík, *Manuale fondamentale di spiritualità*, 12.

thing against which it is no longer able to fight . . . something to which the person says, or rather must say, "You are."[28]

~

If this is the meaning of the spiritual, then what the spiritual life in the Christian tradition is becomes clear. The ancient masters would repeat it: The spiritual life is life in the Holy Spirit. Spiritual people live immersed in the Holy Spirit. Their lives are illuminated by the Holy Spirit in all its dimensions: intellectual, emotional, and sentimental. Their decisive will, their gestures, words, and actions are guided by the Holy Spirit. Their will goes through life sustained by the force and the energy of the Holy Spirit. The spiritual life is not a discipline or an asceticism, it is more than every science. It is an art of harmony with the Holy Spirit, the art of making his presence fruitful in our lives.

> Faith, in the strict sense of the term, is the affirmation of an absolute existence . . . of an unconditioned existence. This absoluteness belongs equally to all that exists in so far as it is.[29]

The spiritual life is the art of being aware of the Holy Spirit. The fundamental act of the spiritual life is the recognition of the Holy Spirit, a recognition so radical as to create a *habitus* of giving precedence to the Spirit, that is, of living in a constant openness to the Other. This openness is a profound awareness that power, life, and wisdom dwell in the Other. It is a deeply religious act. As stated before, the religious principle is the radical recognition of the unconditioned existence of the Other.

---

28. Vjačeslav I. Ivanov, "Anima" (The Soul), in Semyon L. Frank, *Il pensiero religioso russo: Da Tolstoj a Losskij* (Russian Religious Thought: From Tolstoy to Lossky) (Milan: Vita e Pensiero, 1977), 189.

29. Vladimir Solov'ëv, *Kritika otvlečënniych načal* (The Critique of Abstract Principles), in *Sobranie Sočinenii*, vol. 2 (Brussels: Foyer Oriental Chrétien, 1966). Translated into Italian as *La critica dei principi astratti (1877-1880)*, in *Sulla Divinoumanità e altri scritti* (Milan: Jaca, 1971), 203.

The sense of the self placed outside the boundaries of the individual is the starting point of every mysticism, as wonder is for philosophy. . . . Ecstasy is the first moment in every religious life, the alpha and the omega of the religious state.[30]

This act coincides with the Christian understanding of Love. Love means detaching oneself from the affirmation of one's own absoluteness, common to each individual, in order to recognize complete absoluteness in the Other. Love is an ecstatic movement of going out of oneself to recognize the true center in the Other.

Love . . . is the transfer of all our interest in life from ourselves to another, as the shifting of the very center of our personal lives.[31]

This is a going-out that is neither destructive nor alienating, a going-out that is a denial of self, but is at the same time joyful because it is the greatest expression of a Being called Love.

In order to know Love it is necessary to look at God. John, in his first letter, shows that Love is made up of how God loves us. He gave his own Son, who died for us. Christ's paschal event did not destroy God, but rather triumphantly revealed him as Lord of Life.

Recognizing in love the truth of another, not abstractly, but essentially, transferring in deed the center of our life beyond the limits of our empirical personality, we by so doing reveal and realize our own real truth, our own absolute significance, which consists just in our capacity to transcend the borders of our factual phenomenal being, in our capacity to live not only in ourselves, but also in another.[32]

The fact that the religious principle and the principle of Love coincide is no surprise for us Christians — our God is Love. Believing in God

---

30. Vjačeslav I. Ivanov, "Ellinskaia religiia stradajouščego boga" (The Hellenic Religion of the Suffering God), *Vosprosy žizni* 7 (1905): 179.

31. Vladimir Solov'ëv, *Smysl ljubvi*, in *Sobranie Sočinenii*, vol. 7 (Brussels: Foyer Oriental Chrétien, 1966). Translated into English as *The Meaning of Love*, tr. Thomas R. Beyer, Jr. (Hudson, NY: Lindisfarne Press, 1985), 51.

32. Solov'ëv, *The Meaning of Love*, 45.

therefore is not adherence to doctrines nor taking up determined ethical attitudes, but rather it is the recognition of God as Love and the orientation of one's whole life toward him. The exercise of faith is relationship. To believe means to recognize oneself in an existential relationship with the personal God who embraces the whole person, even one's knowledge and moral actions.

The fundamental attitude that characterizes Christian spiritual life is therefore inseparable from faith and from Love. To believe and to love are two inseparable dimensions that constitute a person's mode of existence in the spiritual life.

17. The Trichotomy of the Fathers

In fact, by means of the Father's hands, that is, the Son and the Spirit, the person, and not a part of the person, is made in the image and likeness of God. . . . The perfect person is the mixture and the union of the soul that has received the Father's Spirit, which is mixed into the flesh formed in the image of God.[33]

Those familiar with the Pauline and patristic trichotomy will recognize this vision of the spiritual and the spiritual life. The Fathers said that the person is the unity of the Spirit, body and soul. As in the icon of the Face of Christ, this triple structure can be schematized in three concentric circles.

The spiritual life has its origin in the action of the Holy Spirit who acts from within the person and makes himself manifest to the external world in the lived experience, the action, and the mentality of the Christian. The indwelling of the Holy Spirit in the person is a participation in the Love of God the Father for humanity. This participation is the constitutive act of a person because the creation of the person is the communi-

---

33. Irenaeus, *Adversus haereses,* 5.6.1.

cation of the Love of God, that is, the essence of God, his most personal reality. It is precisely the communication of the personal dimension of God that makes the creature a human person. The Holy Spirit pours into our hearts the Love of God the Father (Rom. 5:5). The agapic principle is at the root of a person's spiritual life. In the interior circle of the design, where the Holy Spirit dwells, it can truly be written "the Love of God."

The agapic dimension of the spiritual can therefore be understood through Love itself. Divine Love is an absolute relational reality, a total reality that includes and embraces all, a personal dynamism that touches everything in existence. In this sense Love is the only absolute idea that it is possible to conceive of, the Living Idea. It is a personal, not a conceptual reality. To think of Love means to think of an organism united with an absolute and inseparable connection. Love is the universal Oneness.

At the same time, this Love is fragile. Love is the only absolute reality that exists as if it did not. Love is an unbreakable relationship and is completely absent. Love succeeds in being present in such a way that the beloved, if he or she wants, can experience it only as pure absence. Love embraces the beloved and at the same time it does not hold the person back but sets the beloved free. Love loves but the beloved one can do without it. It is there, but it does not impose itself. Love can wait forever, even if the beloved ignores it and never welcomes it. Love does not destroy the beloved because it is inseparable from freedom. Love includes freedom. Love does not exist if not in freedom and, vice versa, the real meaning of freedom is grasped only in love.

Separating love from freedom means suppressing both love and freedom. Freedom, as an inner dimension of love, is precisely the dimension that renders love eternal. Freedom in love is the greatest objectivity that human intelligence can comprehend because it makes possible a radical recognition of the other as objectivity "in itself," even to the point of making this objectivity of the other free from any claim placed upon it.

An example of such objectivity is found in Christ on the Mount of Olives, when the Lord recognizes totally the real objectivity of the Father. The same objectivity is seen in the Mother of God at the moment of the Annunciation. This means that it is possible to speak of a true objectivity only upon arriving at the thought that thinks within relationship. Objectivity is what our minds arrive at by means of recognizing the other. Objectivity is recognized, not imagined or projected.

The recognition of the other is so radical that, if it happens that this love is refused, it does not destroy love. Freedom is precisely the reality that makes the loving recognition of the other possible in such a way that the other remains free whether accepting love or not. Either way, love never stops loving. For this reason, tragedy occurs precisely in the freedom at the heart of love. Thus the Crucifixion: The strongest love reaches its greatest height in a recognition of the other so objective that it is capable of accepting the "no," the refusal, and notwithstanding this stands firm and keeps loving. Therefore even the "yes" is true only in the freedom of love and there is, in that same dimension of love, also celebration and the joy of a corresponding and accepted love.

With this characteristic of love communicated to us by the Holy Spirit, God can dwell in us without rivalries, reciprocal threats, or limitations. The relationship between God and humanity is therefore the Love communicated through the Holy Spirit.

18. Uniting and Expansive Love

To be in love with another's personality is to perceive the identity and unity underlying its perpetual change and division; it is to perceive its nobility even in the midst of utter degradation. Love is the means by which the obscurity of the objective world is illuminated and the heart of existence is penetrated, so that the Thou may displace and, finally, annihilate the object.[34]

It could be said that the person lives simultaneously in two registers: in the self and in relationship.[35]

34. Nikolai Berdiaev, *Ja i mir* (Paris: YMCA Press, 1934). Translated into English as *Solitude and Society,* tr. George Reavey (New York: Charles Scribner's Sons, 1939), 196.

35. Dumitru Staniloaë, *Dieu est amour* (God Is Love), tr. Daniel Neeser (Geneva: Labor et Fides, 1980), 32.

～

Love is absolute connectedness, the heart in which all the connections that exist are united. It is the strongest magnetism, even capable of uniting what is impossible according to human logic. The Holy Spirit, as Saint Paul says, gives the Love of God to human hearts, endowing them with the same unifying power. We can, therefore, affirm that the first movement of the spiritual life is centripetal, meaning that it enters into our interiority from without, unifying us.

If the Spirit acts as unifier, this means that the principle of spiritual integration is Love. Only Love, which unifies but does not make uniform, can bring all of a person's contradictions and antinomies, all the mental, emotional, and physical wounds that keep a person divided and suffering, into harmonious agreement. At the same time it rebuilds unity and reaffirms life. Love radiates its expansive, relational dynamism in ecstasy, that is, toward others and toward all creation. This is the second movement of the spiritual life, a centrifugal movement.

This consists of one, unique moment — in itself and in relationship — distinct in two phases only for the sake of rational comprehension. In Love they form a single act, even at the phenomenological level. When the person encounters a particular aspect of another, even physically, it becomes assumed into Love within the workings of Love, becoming Love itself integrated into the person as gift and relationship. When the "other" is loved for a particular quality, it becomes precious because it recalls what makes the person beloved, what distinguishes the "other." Through Love that manifests itself in the particular, I perceive myself as united and whole because another, in loving me, has recognized my particularity.

19. The Spiritual Life Is Christological

The first man, "natural man," was the image and likeness of God; the new "spiritual man" was God himself, for the Being who then appeared was an absolute manifestation who epitomized in himself the true meaning of all that is. In him God is no longer that law which lies heavily on material life. . . . God is greater than that and can do much more than that, as Christ eminently showed when he demonstrated him to be love, or in other words, absolute personality.[36]

Christ the new Adam, in the very revelation of the mystery of the Father and of his love, fully reveals humanity to itself and brings to light its very high calling. . . . Conformed to the image of the Son who is the firstborn of many brothers and sisters, Christians receive the "first fruits of the Spirit" (Rom. 8:23) by which they are able to fulfill the new law of love. By this Spirit, who is the "pledge of our inheritance" (Eph. 1:14), the entire person is inwardly renewed, even to the "redemption of the body" (Rom. 8:23).[37]

The culmination of the spiritual life is in Christ. Christ is the final word on God and humanity, the total and definitive communication of God, and thus the spiritual par excellence.

God is Love. Love is the essence of the divine nature, the life of the Most Holy Trinity, the most spiritual reality. If we wonder what speaks most to us of God, what most reminds us of and bring us closer to him, what best expresses the sense, the intimate knowledge, the taste of God, there is no doubt that the answer is Love. For us, Christ, in all his reality, is Love, the word that narrates the depth of God the Father, the immensity of the goodness of God and his wonders. Christ is the primordial Word of life that remains for us to touch and taste, because in his body he has made that absolute Love that escapes humanity in the abysses of Trinitarian Love visible. Christ is the image of a simple human being, conditioned by history, marked by the events of human life that reveal intelligence, a way of thinking that is filled with Love. The paschal event is the

---

36. Solov'ëv, *God, Man, and the Church*, 114-115.

37. Vatican II, *Gaudium et spes*, 22, in *Vatican Council II: Constitutions, Decrees, Declarations*, tr. Austin Flannery (Northport, NY: Costello Publishing, 1996), 185-186.

pinnacle of the revelation of him who is "Abba," Father. His call to the Father gathers together the last and most profound hope toward which entire generations of the descendants of Adam, lost and bewildered, had been striving for centuries.

The Body of Christ is what is absolutely spiritual in the cosmos and in humanity because it is the word of God, the revelation and communication of God, and our return to him.

In Christ the person is totally spiritual because he is God. Christ on the cross who, through the power of the Holy Spirit, offers himself as an absolute and loving sacrifice is a person completely hypostatized in Love. There is no atom of his person that is not assumed in and lived for Love. All of Christ is consumed in Love. It is in his Passion that the true meaning of the spiritual is founded. Christ, true God and true human: Christ the true human means Christ true God, that is, the Love of the Father. All of the humanity assumed in Christ becomes hypostatized in the person (hypostasis) of the Son, in the filial Love for the one Father, source of Love and of Life. In Christ on the cross the ultimate truth of his humanity is unveiled: his sonship of God the Father.

20. The Eucharistic Dimension of the Spiritual

We thank you for the nourishment you give us through your holy gift. Pour out your Spirit upon us and in the strength of this food from heaven keep us single-minded in your service.[38]

So, my God, I prostrate myself before your presence in the universe which has now become living flame: beneath the lineaments of all that I shall encounter this day, all that happens to me, all that I achieve, it is you I desire, you I await.[39]

38. Prayer after Communion of the Thirty-Second Week in Ordinary Time.
39. Pierre Teilhard de Chardin, *Hymn of the Universe*, tr. Simon Bertholomew (New York: Harper & Row, 1965), 29.

~

The sacrament, as a reality founded by Christ and in Christ in the paschal mystery, is spiritual. The sacrament makes history, creation, and humanity itself Christlike. The realities chosen by Christ — water, bread, wine — become a communication of God in a personal way, that is, in Christ's way. In the sacrament, God loves creation and humanity in a tangible way, precisely as he has loved through his Son, Jesus Christ.

The dogma of the Eucharist offers the authentic meaning of the spiritual and of spiritual life. In the Eucharistic consecration the bread and the wine, two realities that express the fruit of the earth and the work of human hands, through the power of the Holy Spirit become a perfectly spiritual reality, the body and blood of Christ. In the Eucharistic liturgy celebrated by the Church through the ministry of the priesthood, in the gift of the Holy Spirit invoked in the epiclesis, a piece of bread narrates to us the whole history of Christ. It makes all of salvation present to us and communicates to us in a real way the gift that he makes of himself.

Christ breaks the bread and gives it to the disciples. Eating, they destroy it and live, because one must eat in order to live. Christ identifies this bread and this act with himself. The body of Christ offers itself to humanity, allows itself to be abused and destroyed, takes upon itself all of the violence accumulated through the sins of the world. When hanging upon the cross, bloody and spent, he looks at humanity and with his whole person he says, "Taste and see that the LORD is good" (Ps. 34:8). How good is the Lord who allows himself to be so treated by humanity. How much he loves humanity that, even though he knows well that we are sinners, belonging to a perverted and violent generation, he entrusts himself totally into our hands so that we might see that he is truly God and how infinitely good he is. Humanity survives with him because he returns to the Father, ending the exile begun with Adam and beginning the exodus from the deserts, from the arid lands where there is neither water nor life. Humanity receives life from its foundational relationship with the Creator and Father. It is a relationship made possible by Christ crucified, who, revealing that God is Father because he is Love, defeated the false image of God that the ancient serpent had wormed into human hearts. The Christian celebrates the Eucharist and contemplates the gift of God that does not merely *give* but *gives God himself.*

Whoever enters church bringing bread, fruit of the earth, for the offering offers a bread made with worries, sufferings, and problems. It is a bread stained by sin and by the wounds of daily life, which do not speak of God but rather clench the heart with pain. That same person, however, leaves church and returns home with Christ.

As Eucharistic bread, in becoming Christ, narrates the whole story of Christ's sacrifice and love for us, so those things offered together with the bread, once united to Christ, begin to orient a person's heart to him. Even if they are painful, sad realities, if they are repeatedly united to Christ, offered together with the bread become the body of Christ, these difficult and oppressive realities are taken upon the body of Christ, united to him, imprinted on his flesh, as at the hour of the Passion when he took upon himself all of our iniquity.

This does not only consist of a rational operation. Just as bread really nourishes, so that same bread become the body of Christ truly communicates his life, and the chalice involves us in the Paschal Event in such an existential way that the strength of Christ begins to act within us, opening us to his own spiritual dimension. In the Eucharist our offerings live a real transfiguration, just as the body of Christ, which in the Passion took evil upon itself, arose transfigured.

Vladimir Solov'ëv, speaking about beauty, offers the famous example of coal and diamonds. They have the same chemical reality but different physical structures. One, full of internal contradictoriness, does not allow light to pass through but rather eats, devours, kills it. It remains black. The other — the diamond — allows light to shine through it, allows the same substance as coal to become a thing of indescribable beauty.

This example can allow us to comprehend the Christological, Eucharistic, and sacramental dimension of the spiritual. Bread can be the cause of conflict because it is an element to possess, therefore a reality that divides. However, the same bread assumed into the Eucharist, into the body of Christ, imbued with the Love of God, becomes the sacrament of communion, the splendor of creation. In it shines the Truth of creation.

It reflects the face of the Creator who is God the Giver. The human being, the human body, in which are mixed instincts, passions, selfish desires, the will for self-preservation, becomes the fullness of creation, the
true image and likeness of the invisible God in Jesus Christ. Matter, the
body and whatever other reality, once penetrated by Love, appears transfigured, reveals its inner truth. The bread becomes true bread, the drink,
true drink, and humanity, true humanity. The bread receives its inner
truth in the Eucharist when it becomes the communication of Love,
when it is completely hypostatized in Christ.

In these terms it is understandable that the spiritual is not a rational-
istic idealism. It is not humanity that gives a spiritual meaning to things
but the Holy Spirit who reveals the Truth and the ultimate meaning of everything in Love. The surfaces of creation are opened; the appearances of
events are revealed from one side and from the other; Love opens our
hearts and interior eyes to read and welcome spiritual revelation in creation. This is not idealism, because beyond every speculation stands a historical fact, that of the crucifixion and resurrection of Christ in which all
this is made real. Humanity has revealed divinity and divinity has revealed true humanity.

21. Finding God in All Things

*In the third point I will consider how God labors and works for me
in all the creatures on the face of the earth.*[40]

*They can practice seeking the presence of our Lord in everything:
their dealing with other people, their walking, seeing, tasting, hear-
ing, understanding, and all our activities. For his Divine Majesty is
truly in everything by his presence, power, and essence.*[41]

---

40. Ignatius of Loyola, *The Spiritual Exercises and Selected Works*, ed. George E.
Gonss (Mahwah, NJ: Paulist Press, 1991), 177.
41. Ignatius of Loyola, *The Spiritual Exercises*, 353.

Knowledge gravitates around the notion of object, but only love can decentralize us in some way, making us consider the other as subject.[42]

Just as the body, when it tastes the delectable foods of this earth, knows by experience exactly what each thing is, so the intellect, when it has triumphed over the thoughts of the flesh, knows for certain when it is tasting the grace of the Holy Spirit, for it is written: "Taste and see that the Lord is good" (Ps. 34:8). The intellect keeps fresh the memory of this taste through the energy of love, and so unerringly chooses what is best.[43]

In the Eucharistic wake of the spiritual and of the spiritual life, things, both objects and events, light up before us like the burning bush of Moses in the desert.

A rather mechanical, formal logic extended in analysis attracts us with the question: "What is this?" However, the action of the Spirit, with an agapic logic, invites us to kneel, to remove our sandals, to establish a relationship with things, with objects and creation. To the question "What is this?" Love whispers, "Who is here?" Love pushes us to seek the subject in objects and that Pentecostal whisper speaks to the intellect within the heart. The meaning of things can only be known by recognizing, by taking into consideration, by creating relationships. This is the crux of the fundamental attitude of the spiritual life: to give precedence, to take into account. Just as soon as Moses had begun to take the Lord into consideration and to accept the logic of Love — he could not know the Lord if he did not consider him, if he did not take him into account — then God spoke to him. It is impossible to know God without God.

42. Jean LaCroix, *Personne et amour* (Person and Love) (Lyon: Editions du Livre français, 1942), 11.

43. Diadochus of Photiki, *On Spiritual Knowledge and Discrimination: One Hundred Texts*, n. 30, in *Philokalia*, 1.261.

The Holy Spirit, with the logic of Love, assures that objects open themselves up and that from the speaking subject emerge the objects. This is the spiritual dimension.

The ultimate destiny of creation and of history is to become a spiritual reality, a theophanic, Christ-bearing reality. It is the action of the Holy Spirit that moves our senses through the sensible world, arousing in them the knowledge and sense for the spiritual. The same action of the Spirit moves the person who slowly becomes a reality that is transparently spiritual, that is, theophanic and Christ-bearing.

There is an ambiguity in the senses that has caused many misunderstandings of their true meaning in the spiritual life. The senses and everything that has to do with them are easily understood as obstacles to the spiritual life. This is why they are often taught against, using ascetic exercises in order to conquer them. However, the senses are a gift that has been given to the body. They are an integral part of humanity's cognitive system. Their true meaning consists in tasting of the goodness of the Creator; therefore, they have a role to play in the spiritual life.

Every corporeal sense has its twin in the Spirit. An exterior sense has its twin in the interior part of the soul, there where the soul opens itself to the Spirit (if we avail ourselves again of the image of the three circles of the trichotomy). The spiritual life consists in looking with the external eyes and in seeing with internal eyes, with spiritual eyes. It is as if the same reality seen with corporeal eyes were read interiorly as a spiritual reality and becomes that which really is, a reality that says something about God, something that orients us towards him. Progressively, the external and internal senses become one. That which the external senses perceive, interiorly becomes a spiritual sense.

> For unless his [the Holy Spirit's] divinity actively illumines the inner shrine of our heart, we shall not be able to taste God's goodness with the perceptive faculty undivided, that is, with unified aspiration.[44]

It is the fruit of the Holy Spirit's action that, with its interior revelation, becomes the cardinal point for the external senses, orienting them

44. Ibid., n. 29, I.261.

toward their interior twin. Thus the Holy Spirit carries out the work of likeness with God.

22. Even Death and Sin Can Be Spiritual

Christ gave his death to the Father, and so, in Christ, death dies: "trampling down death by death." From that moment on, no one dies alone; Christ dies with him in order to raise him up with him.[45]

❧

We know well, however, how much in human beings rebels against the spiritual. People are continuously tempted to define the confines between what is and what is not spiritual themselves, to decide what constitutes the spiritual life and what is not a part of it.

Besides these classic temptations of gnosticism, there are others, just as classic, such as the temptation of not considering death as spiritual. Death is not just what is conventionally meant by the term, but is also interior, a rupture with God, rebellion against him, self-assertion and pride, that is, sin. It is also everything that plays some part in death and sin, such as failure, defeat, injustice, abuse, derision, misunderstanding. In speaking of the spiritual life we cannot avoid reflecting on this.

In a powerful hand movement, Christ yanks bewildered Adam and Eve from Hades. We have here the *powerful meeting of the two Adams* and a foretelling of the fullness of the Kingdom. The two Adams are together and identify with one another, no longer in the *kenosis* of the Incarnation but in the Glory of the Parousia. "He who said to Adam 'Where are you?' has mounted the Cross to search for him who was lost. He went down into Hades saying: Come to me my image and my likeness" (a hymn by St. Ephrem). . . . "And the Lord extended his hand and made the sign of the cross on Adam and all the saints. And taking

45. Paul Evdokimov, *The Art of the Icon: A Theology of Beauty,* tr. Steven Bigham, (Torrance, CA: Oakwood Publications, 1990), 313.

Adam by the hand, he rose up out of Hades, and all the saints followed him." Christ does not come out of the tomb but out from "among the dead," *ek nekron*. . . .[46]

Humanity descended from Adam, descended from Cain, and, after the tragic experience of sin, flees before the Face of the Lord and takes refuge in the tomb. The empire of death and hell becomes a safe refuge. If God cannot enter the tomb, the reverse is also true; death cannot become a spiritual reality, death cannot speak of God, the dead do not sing the praises of the Lord.

To arrive at the tomb it is necessary to pass through that which precedes it. Sin caused death; therefore, it cannot become a spiritual reality. Thinking this way, humanity is in some way convinced that the tomb is a place at which God cannot arrive. For that reason, the human kingdom is the place in which we believe ourselves to be the sole masters. Sin consists precisely in this error. In Christ, however, God entered the tomb and took upon himself the world's sin. The tree of Eden on which humanity fixed its gaze, taking it off of God, is in fact a trap, a bait that attracts with great and false promises. Divinization, the attributes of the Absolute, the Beautiful, the Good, and Knowledge, that is, Truth, were expected from that tree. Instead, its fruit brought only death, from generation to generation.

God did not forget humanity, which had forsaken him for the tree. So, in order to be taken into consideration once again, he comes himself, descending in person and allowing himself to be nailed to the wood of that tree upon which the idolatrous eyes of humanity were fixed. Only thus could humanity, whose gaze had become fossilized in its sin from which life was expected, see the face of the Creator, which was now also the face of the Savior. In sin, which turns persons into mere objects, the face of the Person could now be seen, once more allowing humanity the ability for hypostatization, to become his sacred image.

People continue to sin. We sin anyhow, expecting that sin will provide some relief, some profit, some conquest, maybe redemption. Thus,

---

46. Ibid., 324-325.

after every sin the deceit is greater, the night darker. The tree-of-sin makes humanity into an object because it is an object itself. Therefore, it is on an object-tree that the agapic principle, the personal principle, Love, had to allow itself to be nailed so that human beings, enslaved by objects, might return again to being persons, so that we might raise our gaze from a culture of objects and of things to a culture of the heart, of relationships, and of communication.

> In reality we understand God, actually we even conceive of him, in our sinfulness. Our hand, clenched to take and to kill, encloses the gift that holds forgiveness and resurrection for us. It is the great mystery of our salvation, the only encounter possible between us and God with full respect for the freedom of both.[47]

It is from sin, in which God let himself be imprisoned, that the word is once again spoken to humanity. It is a word of resurrection, just as God created humanity in speaking the Word, so now he recreates humanity, resurrecting us. God the Father has made him who has not sinned into sin for us (2 Cor. 5:21). I think this Pauline expression is one of the most shocking words of the New Testament: The Holy God, faithful and omnipotent, makes himself sin in order to reach humanity that lies in sin. As the serpent in the desert brings death, so gazing upon the serpent of Moses brings life. Even sin and death speak of God in Jesus Christ because Christ burdens his own shoulders with our reality. He covered himself with humanity's crime and from there he has spoken to us.

Just to reopen dialog with humanity, Christ lets himself be driven to death and into the tomb in order to surprise us in our final hiding place where we had sought refuge, escape from the living God, sure that death could not speak of life or communicate God. However, even this human vision of death, like sin, reveals itself to be a deception.

Christ who in his incarnation descends into the abyss of hell is the

---

47. Silvano Fausti, *Ricorda e racconta il Vangelo: La catechesi narrativa di Marco* (Recalling and Recounting the Gospel: The Narrative Catechesis in Mark) (Milan: Àncora, 1989), 481-482. This is a comment on Mark 14:48: "Have you come out with swords and clubs to arrest me as if I were a bandit?"

culmination of his revelation, his clearest word, the most explicit and well-defined image of God. He communicates God in death, in the tomb, and in the resurrection.

The spiritual life therefore is also an initiation of the Holy Spirit to the spiritual reading of the most tragic human dimensions and a revelation of their spiritual sense.

Is it really possible to arrive at this?

If loving is like creating a child, forgiving is like raising someone from the dead.[48]

The answer in the spiritual life consists in forgiveness.

Those who discover themselves to be sinners feel all the weight and the darkness of sin. They know how thoughts obsessively turn to the places of sin and to the sin committed. Sometimes this is a sudden awareness. They feel a great fear, as if a bird of ill omen crossed their heart, and what they have done reveals its burdensome and disturbing face of evil. They are no longer able to escape. Memory is exposed as wounded, weighted down, as if nailed to a painful monster from which it is impossible to get away. Forgetting is beyond our human capacity. Wicked memories of sin fill the heart with anguish, worry, rage, and rancor.

The only one who can free us from this memory is the one who says, as written in Jeremiah, *"I will forgive their iniquity and remember their sin no more"* (31:34).

Sinners who encounter the One who forgives can finally forget the anguish of sin, and they will always remember the One who has forgiven them. The memory, once wounded and nailed to evil, is cured and transfigured into a memory of good, or rather, of the good, because it becomes a memory of the Savior.

Sin does not become a spiritual reality until it is separated from God. The dynamic of sin forces the sinner to flee far from God and neighbor. Forgiveness instead reunifies and heals, creating an insoluble connection between sin and the Redeemer-King. The forgiveness that unites sin to

48. Silvano Fausti (ed.), *Una comunità legge il vangelo di Luca* (A Community Reads the Gospel of Luke), vol. 1 (Bologna: EDB-Edizioni Dehoniane, 1986), 195.

the Person of the Redeemer carries out the transfiguration of the memory and of the mind.

The sin can no longer be remembered without recalling God. If the memory again returns to sin it is only to glorify the Lord who has taken it upon himself. When the beauty of the Lord and his merciful gaze inebriates the soul, sin becomes a spiritual reality, a reality that orients one toward God. In forgiving, God communicates himself to the sinner and sin ceases to be a dark, putrefied reality that alienates one from life and relationship.

Christian tradition tells us of saints whose hearts, while praying, wept sweetly because, in recognizing their own sin, they felt overcome by the sweetness of God's mercy, inebriated by forgiveness, overwhelmed with joy in the celebration of their return to the Father.

In this light, the penance that penitents receive becomes a spiritual medicine that helps them to keep the memory of forgiveness, the perennial memory of the Savior's loving gaze, upon them. Forgiven sinners conquer sin and leave behind their sinful life now that sin, no longer separated from Christ, has become the cornerstone of the spiritual life that they begin to build with Christ. Humanity distances itself from sin mainly because it has come to know the good Father, the loving God, and we no longer flee from him but, on the contrary, run towards him. Whoever complains against repentant sinners, continuing to consider them as they were before being forgiven, is not a spiritual person. Those who do not consider the sinner with the forgiveness that God has given are only ethical ideologues whose dogmatic judgment of the other reveals the fact that they consider themselves god. Mercy shown to sinners, compassion for them, is the clearest sign of the spiritual life. At times there are those who hide cruel and fossilized judgments about people behind pious phrases and quotes from Sacred Scripture. In reality this indicates hardness of heart and stubbornness *(philautia)*. Thus ethical norms and spiritual theories are separated from life and torn from the total vision of the person or else they are tied to specific persons who, in a sectarian style, become the norms and judges of good and evil.

23. Psychological Reality Tends toward the Spiritual

The entire complexity of our human nature that comes from our dramatic history, from the failures and the brilliances of our freedom, every ambiguity of the "garments of skin," by now transfigured, will find a place in the kingdom. Actually, we marvel that the empty caves dug out by our freedom in the goodness of creation in Christ have become those wounds of the hands, the feet, the heart, through which, for all times, divine life reaches and will reach us.[49]

Praying for inner healing means, first of all, permitting Jesus to visit all those areas of our life in which we have been wounded. . . . At the root of a wound there is a problem of forgiveness. It is, therefore, a spiritual problem.[50]

∾

In pastoral work I have noticed that failures and sufferings of whatever type are great obstacles along the journey of the spiritual life. Every personal story leaves its marks on the psyche. Moreover, there are persons who have had a fragile mind from birth, sometimes even a damaged one. All these realities are in and of themselves very close to Christ, intimately tied to his paschal drama.

Often, however, it is a formal and idealist culture that warps and blinds us, impeding us from seeing the relationship between our wounds and traumas and the drama of our Lord's Passion. It can make us incapable of accepting the word of God that comes to us but which is already within our hearts.

As I have said above, it is often heard said that there is a need to heal the psyche, to liberate oneself from one's own personal history before be-

49. Olivier Clément, *Questions sur l'homme* (Questions on Humanity) (Paris: Editions Stock, 1972), 206.
50. N. Astalli Hidalgo and A. Smets, *Sauver ce qui était perdu* (Saving the One Who Was Lost) (Paris: Saint-Paul, 1986), 27.

ginning to work on the spiritual life. It seems to me that the fundamental question is another, but it cannot be understood without entering into the dimension of the Love of God.

I mean to say that even psychological suffering, even a disorder in our personal make-up, even a failure can communicate God, can become a remembrance of God and our participation in his Passion.

The sacramental dimension of the Church can illuminate this journey very well. A wounded person, incapable either by make-up or nature of turning to God or of establishing peaceful relationships with others, can experience love, caring, and attention in a community of Christians. If it happens that someone, as a brother or sister, lovingly recognizes another's existence, perhaps the same story will be repeated a thousand times, perhaps that other will cry out bitterly, but in this relationship, even though continuing to suffer, that suffering will slowly be mitigated through the one reaching out to the other. That pain, lived within a relationship of charity, then begins to recall the community, the Church, and relationships of love and of freedom to them. Where there is charity, there is God.

Those who suffer, or who are victims of their own sicknesses, will be able to concretely experience that being aware of their own make-up and psychological wounds is not everything. What is truly important is to lovingly acknowledge our psychological world, unknown or unrecognized, so that we might welcome, accept, and wholeheartedly entrust it to God.

After all, it is not so important to reach a psychological tranquility. Even that can be an idol and so should not be mythologized. What counts and what is really healthy is discovering that our lives are gathered and hidden with Christ in God. Rationally, I can eliminate those episodes of my past that make me suffer. I can refuse to recognize them and live as a psychological invalid, just as I can accept them, "normalize" myself, and live in "tranquility." If all that I am and have been, however, is not gathered and integrated into Love, I remain just half a person because there is a whole part of my past, of my person, that has not been gathered into eternal Love. It is necessary that I find a way to see these events transfigured in Christ for eternity.

Prayer, a fundamental dimension of the spiritual life, has an enormous importance in all this. Recognizing, before the Lord, our good and also evil thoughts, our joyful or violent emotions, it is possible to concretely live a moment of welcoming and acceptance. We can present them to the word of God repeatedly or just tell them to the Lord simply calling him by name. Normally they are things that one does speaking to oneself in a mental soliloquy. The true examination of conscience that saves is to consign these realities to the Other. It is not the same if I free myself from my thoughts and feelings through professional dialogue or in a spiritual relationship when the other links these things to Christ, because what is needed is not a throwing away of our thoughts but a spiritualization of them. This does not mean repressing or covering up our realities but learning to live in the freedom of relationship with him in whom all our things are purified.

The separation or confusion of the psychological and the spiritual is due to a picture of spirituality that does not truly succeed in integrating pain and suffering. It is as if it were difficult to include what is not rationally controllable or what is not part of a reassuring image of life in the spiritual. This is a deeply conditioned distortion of formal idealistic logic, which impedes one from accepting the truth of the Love of God. The display and fulfillment of God's Love have no determined, privileged, or a priori forms.

God is thought of as absolute perfection, and in the incarnation he appears to us as such. This perfection, however, is to be understood in a formal sense. God's perfection consists in his Holiness, which is Love. Through Divine Love, with the historical incarnation of God in Jesus Christ, any scenario of human history becomes an extraordinary occasion of fulfillment, even the form of a slave or a criminal. It is at the moment of the crucifixion that the fulfillment of Love is complete.

We have to rethink the problem of suffering and the fact that only someone in perfect mental form can grow spiritually. In Love, psyche and spirit unite. Participating in the suffering and death of Christ and the experience of the strength of the resurrection are much more present in the toils of daily life than we are accustomed to think. We must not forget that at Golgotha, from the point of view of formal logic, Christ lived a complete failure, while from the point of view of Love it is the moment of triumph over death and evil. It is legitimate to think that suffering, either physical or mental, when seen from the outside, can only be a reality of suffering. Seen from within, however, through the eyes of God's Love that suffers and rises in that person, it becomes a very different reality.

Human mentality finds its truth in the relational dimension. It expresses all its potentiality and reaches the fulfillment of its complete truth in relationship with others. The human psyche is perfected and spiritualized in that it is assumed in the agapic principle, in the principle of hypostatization. Only the Love of God knows the truth of how much a reality is hypostatized, or involved in agape. Only Christ, in whom the whole human psyche was hypostatized in agape, knows the true meaning of all of humanity's psychological situations.

In every question we wind up colliding with formal logic, with suffocating norms that we ourselves have imposed on our rapports and relationships. A fragile, suffering, or unbalanced psyche embarrasses us because those disfigured by suffering do not correspond to the formally perfect ideal of our idealistic psychological categories. However, it is not at all certain that a psyche is healthy when it corresponds to the norms that we have established. It is healthy and whole when it lives in the sphere of relationship and when it includes itself and the world in the process of hypostatization, when it lives in the Love of God.

There remain two very brief clarifications regarding the intellect and feelings that show that there is no contradiction between the various spheres of the human person. There is no antagonism between the intellect and feelings. Feelings are not external to the intellect, but are part of the rational dimension. Reason *(ratio)* and feeling *(affectus)* are two dimensions of the mind *(intellectus)*. Any type of antagonism between the two, therefore, is a falsification of reality.

Even the spiritual life and the intellect are inseparably united. The human intellect is the crux of the spiritual life. In a sense it can even be said that the spiritual life does not exist outside of the intellect. Here we are speaking of the intellect in the noble sense that the ancients gave it, the intellect that delves into the ontological abysses of the human heart. Each of the intellect's activities, if illuminated by the spiritual depths of the heart and guided by agape, leads to complete spiritual knowledge. Rationality and the spiritual life cannot be rivals. One cannot prevail over the other for they reciprocally work one upon the other. The spiritual life is also recognized by a certain common sense with which spiritual people know how to distinguish and make decisions regarding themselves and others. When it concerns others and the capacity to counsel, it can be more spiritual to seek out a person characterized by common sense and judgment than another renowned for holiness. If it is a holiness that has not been tested by life it might only be a fluke or some particular individual's will of which we have already spoken.

In the past there was often the risk of identifying the spiritual life with rationalism and intellectualism. There was also, as exists mainly today, the risk of identifying it with feeling and sentimentality. Identifying the spiritual life with our feelings leads us to dogmatize the states of our soul and to favor a sort of fanaticism under the pretense of what is good and religious. Spiritual sentimentalism leads to a fatal fragility in the spiritual life and impedes discernment and thus every reading of the truth of facts, events, and persons.

The true spiritual life can be carried out completely even during long periods of sentimental drought when nothing powerful or explicit is "felt" if not a profound awareness of relationship with the Lord which one tries to live in fidelity and expectation. Concentrating too much on our own feelings can prevent us from entering into Easter and understanding the wisdom of the cross and therefore of the true Christ.

Some Verifying Criteria of the Spiritual Life

24. There Is No Division in Love

"God is love and in the Saints the Holy Spirit is love." Dwelling in heaven, the Saints behold hell and embrace it, too, in their love.[51]

Those who have attained the Kingdom of Heaven and abide in God, in the Holy Spirit behold every abyss of hell for there is no domain in all that exists where God could not be. "The whole paradise of Saints lives by the Holy Spirit, and from the Holy Spirit nothing in creation is hid."[52]

~

Spiritual people have a gaze of love upon them. Since Love means complete unity, a living organism in contact with every part of the whole, even spiritual people develop a consciousness of themselves as ever more integrated realities. Loving oneself means considering oneself in a global sense, not overemphasizing a single dimension or dividing oneself up into separate parts or making a single aspect of oneself stand for the whole. To love oneself means to see the meaning of each thing in relation to the entire person.

The same is true of love toward another. Spiritual people seek to live charity toward God because they have experienced the Divine Love that has reached out and redeemed them. This becomes the unique desire of the heart for whoever has entered into the Love of God. Loving God means finding the self in him with everyone, in him and by means of his Love, in Christ, reaching every person on the earth. Spiritual persons do not know particular loves but know Love, and for that reason know the unity of the virtues and the insignificance of actions divorced from Love. If by nature they are led to live one virtue more than any another, they

51. Archimandrite Sophrony (Sakharov), *St. Silouan the Athonite,* tr. Rosemary Edwards (Crestwood, NY: St. Vladimir's Seminary Press, 1999), 116.
52. Ibid.

suffer for what is lacking and it pains them, making them participate in the cross. This suffering is the measure of the maturity of Love, almost a test of its ecclesial nature.

25. Love Needs Matter

Love is that force that drives every being to make an effort in the material world to realize itself.[53]

~

The most serious delusion in the spiritual life consists of the illusion and deceit of oneself. It is possible to think oneself spiritual even when it is not so. We think we have put ourselves into a relationship, that we have gone out of ourselves, crossed the boundaries of our own ego, but this outreach exists only in the mind. We think we have recognized the existence of the other without realizing that the other is not seen objectively, personally, but rather only as a projection of our own self and therefore not as a real person.

Today much is said about relationships. We try courses and undergo relationship therapies, but it is not easy to find someone who truly recognizes the objectivity of the other. As long as we are among friends everything is fine, but when the other reveals aspects of the self that are not pleasing, then the relationship begins to deteriorate irreversibly. The truly spiritual attitude, as we have seen, does not give precedence to one's own psychological categories but to the Holy Spirit recognized as the primary author. It is precisely the transformation, or better, the transfiguration of our lives that reveals the authenticity of the spiritual life because the Holy Spirit's action in the history of creation and of salvation is the transfiguration of the world and of persons. The life of someone who is truly guided by the Holy Spirit becomes ever more Christlike, *de facto*. The Love of God that the person participates in through the Holy Spirit pushes the individual toward transfiguration. In the Holy Spirit, love hypostatizes the

53. LaCroix, *Personne et amour*, 13.

human nature of that person, but the hypostatization of the flesh, of nature, of inherited realities, and of all that the person is means the person being completely open to Love, allowing the self to be shaped by it.

Love needs matter, needs the nature in which to realize itself as Person. The person is not an abstract concept because he or she is constituted by, founded on, Love, and Love is always concrete. The agapic principle is the principle of history, of concreteness, and of duty. The measure of the spiritual life, therefore, is the spiritual concreteness of daily lived experience. It is in daily life that people can see whether their way of thinking conforms to charity: if they shine and rejoice in their body and gestures because they are living an existence of Love. A true spiritual director is never indifferent to a person's social and economic problems. Every detail of a person's life is of interest because the true spiritual director knows that everything has been created to be assumed into the Person, into Love. This is why a spiritual director willingly listens to how a person lives life in its daily details. The world only finds its true meaning and ultimate destiny in Love. Every least part of the cosmos, once given, remains for eternity.

The progressive spiritualization of the world and of life leads to the fulfillment of beauty.[54] *In a theological sense, beauty is a world transfigured by Love, a world in which many realities exist in harmony. The spiritual esthetic is an index of true spiritual life and of a profound comprehension of the spiritual. This is why spiritual persons can make the world beautiful; their presence indelibly marks the social life, politics, and ecology of the times in which they live. Love is a visible word, just as the spiritual person is visible. Love is eternal, just as the spiritual person is eternal, having passed from death to life because of love for brothers and sisters.*

26. The Spiritual Life in Humility

Fasting and abstinence, vigil and withdrawal into silence, and other exploits of spiritual discipline all help, but humility is the principal

---

54. Cf. Micheline Tenace, *La beauté: Unité spirituelle dans les écrits esthétiques de Vladimir Soloviev* (Beauty: Spiritual Unity in the Esthetic Writings of Vladimir Solov'ëv) Troyes: Éditions Fates, 1993).

power. Mary of Egypt subdued her body within a year — there in the desert there was nothing for her to eat — but for seventeen years she had to wrestle against intrusive thoughts. Humility is not learned in a trice. That is why the Lord said, "Learn of me; for I am meek and lowly in heart." Learning takes time. And there are some who have grown old in the practice of spiritual endeavor yet still have not learned humility, and they cannot understand why things are not well with them, why they do not feel peace and their souls are cast down.[55]

❧

The spiritual attitude is one of listening. The spiritual life shapes the human heart in docility. In spiritual anthropology, such as we find it in Sacred Scripture, docility is the fundamental dimension of humility. It does not consist of a psychological humility tempered by the will, which can have a pharisaic end, nor in a depersonalizing humility that renders one insecure even so far as to undermine a person's mental and inner health. We are speaking about humility in a spiritual-theological sense in which humble people are the ones who do not find anything certain in themselves to lean on because their only certainty is the Love that the Other has poured out into them. It is the Word that the Other has written within them and that mysteriously raises them up.

Mary is so poor that she does not find any infallible certainty within herself, but she is completely intent upon her Lord and has given precedence to him. She gives him the first word. She is not sterile, she is a Virgin, that is, she has renounced being the creator of life and had entrusted everything to him. Like a humble servant she looks to the Lord, and that is why their gazes can meet. A basic openness toward the Lord has made her docile to his Word, which is beyond her powers of understanding. This humility of hers is the authentic attitude of the spiritual life, that which makes others feel at home because they have had room made for them and have been made to live. The Virgin remains the incomparable

55. Sophrony (Sakharov), *St. Silouan the Athonite*, 481.

image of this spiritual maturity. She makes herself so docile that in her the Word can become flesh. When we are no longer afraid of disappearing if we give up a place, when we conquer the fear of losing ourselves, of ending up in oblivion if we make ourselves small for the other, only then do we enter into the eternal memory of him to whom we have offered up the space, of him to whom we have offered ourselves. Mary made room for her Lord and he remembered her and her gesture for eternity, assuming her maternal body into heaven. Just as Mary in her maternity made space for the Lord, so he did not abandon her to the oblivion of death but makes her to live with him forever.

A person's spiritual life is recognized by others — we were saying — because Love can only be recognized by those who are loved. This Marian humility is the sign that those who live it are not seeking something for themselves. Those ones whom God has caused to be with his humility pass into his memory because they make present the likeness of the Lord before him in memory of the gesture, the word, the thought with which he made them feel accepted.

However, it is also true that a spiritual person can live unknown forever. It has never been said that an authentic spiritual life is always perceived as such. This recognition will really be possible "only" in eternity, but since the Church as communion will also be there to recognize it, some signs should already be seen here. Even in the case of someone who in this life is not accepted or who is rejected, a trustworthy sign of true spirituality is this person's non-hatred of others.

The criterion for the recognition of the spiritual life on the part of others, therefore, is only one of the possible verifications. The other is the silent confirmation that God gives to the heart of his faithful servant. It is the intuitive certainty of walking upon God's path. It is a certainty that is not stubbornness or outspoken affirmation but which flowers with certainty in the heart like a loving gift from which an unexpected sureness is scattered, a readiness for martyrdom and at the same time an immense humility. It is a humility that succeeds in transfiguring even the aversion of those who do not understand, who err, and above all, the solitude of the misunderstood faithful person into something positive.

On the contrary, precisely because such a life is consumed in hidden and unappreciated fidelity, it becomes a burning bush in the world, the paschal mystery. It is a bush that we become aware of only when the sacrifice is consumed.

27. Love for One's Enemies

This love for one's enemies is agape, the same infinite love with which God loves us, and it is God himself.[56]

~

Love as a relational attitude toward the entirety of the other cannot be produced of itself through an act of will, forcing oneself to love. Yes, it is possible to force oneself to love, and it might last a while, but then comes time to settle accounts. We demand a reimbursement for what has been done for the other, expecting a "salary," or at least a recognition of our efforts, a word of thanks. Love that is forced is a commercial love that resembles slavery. It is a temptation into which parents often fall: "We have sacrificed everything for you, and you give nothing. You want to do however you please and never think about us."

This is not Love. Love is the most explicit demonstration of our kinship to God. It is the particle of God that all people carry within and which leads them to the path of true Love. It is a long path that can start from simple human love but which gets lost in the inscrutability of Trinitarian love because it is beyond asceticism, beyond an act of the will. It is a pure gift to be welcomed with wonder and trembling, in which we must involve ourselves completely. It is love toward those who have done evil to us.

A love for one's enemies is an index of the mature spiritual life. Only within the love of God is it possible to love those who have hurt us, to rejoice sincerely and to thank the Lord for the success of those who have offended us. Only the omnipotence of the Holy Spirit can do this, an om-

56. Fausti (ed.), *Una comunità legge il vangelo di Luca*, 195.

nipotence that transfigures the mind making it like Christ's, who offered himself into our hands while we were yet enemies of God.

28. The Wisdom of the Cross

We are within death and he has descended here, he who can say, "I am life." This is the reason why his death was an inconceivable tearing which encompasses all the world's evil and all our deaths. In this way all anguish, hatred, separation, death, and all our deaths are cancelled, or rather, overthrown, with the same force, in faith, in love, in unity, and in life from him, in the One who was obedient to the Father, obedient even unto death. He, consubstantial with the Father and the Spirit in Trinitarian completeness, was made consubstantial with us even to hell so that even our hell, even our death would refill our freedom, as soon as it lets itself be bent, with light. Hell and death undergo a metamorphosis through him who, abandoning himself to his sovereign compassion, introduces a love stronger than death into the spiritual place where hatred, pride, and despair challenge the kingdom of the separator. Thus, in one sole movement, the Christ breaks the seal of the tombs and the gates of hell.[57]

The spiritual life includes the spiritual understanding of the cross that is, inevitably, encountered in life. Having a balanced relationship with the cross is truly a spiritual art. It does not mean seeking it, or bragging about it, or punishing oneself with a cross, or making oneself a hero helping others at all costs to carry theirs.

When people are facing the cross, many behaviors that indicate an unclear or even unhealthy spirituality can arise. People can think it obligatory, in order to make themselves holy, to choose the path in life that is most marked by the cross. They may think themselves similar to Christ

57. Clément, *Questions sur l'homme*, 203.

by going in search of suffering. Then they slide into spiritual pride. How can someone choose to carry the cross alone if the Son of God, embracing the cross, trembled and asked the Father if it were possible to avoid it? What spiritual presumption is there behind someone who chooses his or her own *via crucis* in order to be perfect and Christlike if the Son of God on the cross cried out to God for having abandoned him?

Around the cross therefore are many hidden traps and deceptions for the spiritual life that are sometimes only disguised psychological games. The wisdom of the cross, instead, is an index of those guided by the Holy Spirit. The wisdom of the cross means welcoming the love that the Holy Spirit gives and being aware that it is through this love that one enters into a paschal logic because whoever loves suffers. Exposing oneself to love and lovingly writing the story of existence, one inevitably enters into the cross. The wisdom of the cross is the reversal of the world's logic. Love gives the strength to sacrifice one's very attachment to all that one holds dear. It gives the capacity to offer up everything. Everything that is given remains forever, which is why the logic of the cross is the logic of resurrection.

29. The Culture of Recognition (Many Cultures, Ethnicities, and Races Living Together)

The Christian attitude towards the world can never be one of nega-tion, whether ascetic or eschatological. The Christian attitude is al-ways affirmation, but an eschatological one: a constant surpassing towards the end that, rather than closing, opens everything to the be-yond.[58]

∼

Another verification of the spiritual life occurs within the cultural arena, or rather, in the multicultural arena.

58. Paul Evdokimov, *L'amour fou de Dieu* (God's Crazy Love) (Paris: Editions du Seuil, 1973), 129.

In itself, culture has a spiritual dimension because culture means sharing and communication and we have seen that everything that is oriented toward the other and that leads to communication is spiritual. The risk for culture is that it might close in on itself, become fossilized, or think itself complete because then it loses the energy of the movement towards others, its force of communication begins to lessen.

In the same way though, whoever keeps alive a spiritual attitude of recognition of the other remains alive culturally as well. Spiritual people establish the same attitude of interior attention towards others that they have toward the Holy Spirit. That means an attention to, a recognition of, and a taking into account of the other. All this is carried out through communication. When I truly communicate with others, I really recognize them, even to the point of handing myself over and communicating myself to them.

The heart of culture is precisely the religious attitude that, with the strength of love, moves a person to communicate. A spiritual person is therefore culturally alive, becoming a principle of openness and communion in a culture that tends toward universal communion. A spiritual person is in continual cultural dialog. They know that no culture is absolute in its concrete, historic manifestation. Such people know that the only absolute of culture is represented in the values and meanings expressed in the recognition of the other and in the search for communication. They know how to discern the essential from the accidental in culture, the true from the artificial. Basically, the spiritual person knows that the words, gestures, and everything that makes up the cultural tapestry can be saved only if placed at the service of dialog and of recognition of others.

True culture, therefore, is the environment that allows us to love our neighbor. It is not possible to recognize the entirety of the other unless there is also a cultural involvement, a "cultural love." The culmination of cultural love is to die to one's own cultural expression for the other, to allow even our own cultural makeup to pass with Christ into Easter.

Spiritual people know that what they renounce out of love for the other will rise again with Christ at the end of time. Languages will die, and only if they have entered into Christ will they rise again. The languages that at the end of time will be recognized by the ones who were loved in those languages will enter into him. Spiritual people know that there is something eternal in their culture that is not to be defended by violence or protected by exclusivity because violence and exclusivity are the assassins of culture. Spiritual people know that they are culturally alive in the measure in which they are open to that interior force of love that keeps them directed toward the other in communication. They know that every cultural particularity they hold dear can also be a dangerous idol that can be placed between themselves and the other. That is why spiritual people know in their hearts that it is more important to remain open and in relationship with the other even if that means giving up their own cultural practices. More important, in fact, is Love, which will raise from the dead all those practices that may have been renounced in order to maintain a relationship with the other. Culture is the phenomenon that most directly recalls the paradox of love. If we want to keep what is most precious and beautiful to us, we must live entirely within the paschal logic of love.

30. Vocation-Resurrection

So then rejoice always in the Lord, all you servants of God. Recognize this first sign of the Lord's love.[59]

All beings and things that our love causes to participate in his presence will also have a place in the new Jerusalem.[60]

Another criterion that can help verify an authentic spiritual life is the question of vocation.

59. Climacus, *The Ladder of Divine Ascent*, 78.
60. Clément, *Questions sur l'homme*, 206.

The beginning of the spiritual life is finding ourselves touched by Christ. Encountering Christ at the place and time in which we least expect him, perhaps even in our sin, is the surprising discovery of the loving God. It is a gift that fills us with wonder and gratitude for the Savior who descends in person to free the beloved. Spiritual life begins precisely in the recognition of the concrete action of God within ourselves and signals the end of a merely abstract and theoretical knowledge of him.

Let us return for a moment to the plan of the trichotomy. The beginning of the spiritual life coincides with the awareness of God's love that, through the Holy Spirit, seeks to penetrate our entire mental and corporeal world in order to reach even the world around us. In this lies the mystery of the will of God and of Christian vocation. It is God's will that the world realizes itself to be loved by him and to return to him. The Christian vocation is the response to this word, the conforming to this will. To respond means to seek the way in which God's love could more easily, more completely, more radically penetrate the person and overflow from the person so that others might perceive it.

Living one's vocation means living according to the agapic principle and therefore continually dying to every attachment, self-assertion, and selfishness. Living one's vocation, therefore, means rescuing one's very body and person from death with the power of the love given by the Holy Spirit. Everything that is "invaded" by Love passes over to resurrection. Allowing one's own person to be pierced by love means engraving on the body made by human hands those signs that will make the individual recognizable after the resurrection, just as Christ, nailed to the tree at the moment of absolute love, is recognized by the disciples because of the marks of those nails.

A true spiritual life is a life to be resurrected. Therefore it is a life that is serene and peaceful, because a vocation that is lived spiritually leads to a healthy humor towards oneself and the events of one's life. A healthy sense of humor could make up a whole other area of discussion and should not be underestimated as a sign of spiritual maturity. I am using "humor" in the sense of accepting things and oneself with that distance that is typical of love that is there, but is as if it were not.

31. *Discernment*

Those pursuing the spiritual way must always keep the mind free from agitation in order that the intellect, as it discriminates among the thoughts that pass through the mind, may store in the treasuries of its memory those thoughts which are good and have been sent by God, while casting out those which are evil and come from the devil.[61]

~

Whoever thinks according to formal logic believes that the spiritual life is an ideal to be accomplished. Instead, as we have seen, it is a process that does not have to do with a formally reachable goal but rather with a living, personal organism that cannot be made abstract. It consists of a dynamism that, the more radical it is, the more perfect it is. This radicality should not be understood here in the sense of a drastic or heroic gesture but as a radical orientation towards Christ with the entire surge of the Spirit that gives love. This means that many formal realizations, completely different from the spiritual life, are possible. True spiritual life reaches maturity through the art of discernment. The discernment of love is actually the guarantee of the health of the spiritual life.

I myself have witnessed what fragility, what psychological weakness, what deviations can intervene in people, especially the young, who embark on a spiritual journey. They can fall prey to fundamentalism, integralism, fanaticism because they understand Sacred Scripture only in one way, or because they dogmatize a feeling, or because they exchange the first thought that crosses their mind for the voice of God. All this and more can happen if we do not make a serious effort in discerning events, encounters, and readings, if we do not learn to discern between thoughts and feelings that lead to Christ and those that distance us from him. Discernment is what makes the journey safe from risks, miscues, and exaggerations.

61. Diadochus of Photiki, *On Spiritual Knowledge*, n. 26, 1.259.

The one who tries to pray only on the basis of what he has heard said or has learned gets lost just as one who has no guide.[62]

The holy Fathers refer to many who entered into the practice of prayer in an incorrect way, following methods for which they were neither sufficiently mature nor capable, and who fell into a spiritual blindness and were attacked by mental turmoil.[63]

A healthy spiritual life can begin in the Church together with others. There we can walk the spiritual path in the company of others, in a spiritual friendship, or at least in the love of a spiritual director. To venture out alone into the spiritual depths means risking being sidetracked or becoming lost. Whoever enthusiastically enters into the spiritual life but does not accept a guide can end up deluded, embittered, even faithless because that person will not have known how to proceed beyond the obstacles, illusions, and deceptions that will certainly be encountered along the way. However, it is also possible that the Holy Spirit himself leads that person from within so that he or she matures without any external help. In history we have always had the so-called "God-taught," that is, those whom God has taught directly. That this does not mean dreamers or enthusiasts can be verified with all that has been said.

Conclusion

I do not claim to have made an exhaustive treatise on the spiritual life, but I wanted to highlight those points of the Christian spiritual life and the meaning of the spiritual that I believe are indispensable for understanding it and that, at the same time, are of great importance for people today. All of this begins from the basis of the truth of humanity, participation in the

---

62. Gregory the Sinaite, in *La filocalia*, ed. M. B. Artioli and M. F. Lovato (Turin: Gribaudi, 1985), 601.

63. Ignatiy Briančaninov, *Sočinenja Episkopa Ignatija* (St. Petersburg, 1905), translated into Italian as *Preghiera e lotta spirituale* (Prayer and Spiritual Struggle) (Turin: Gribaudi, 1991), 146.

life of Trinitarian love. From this excursus it becomes evident that the spiritual life cannot be distanced from an authentic meaning of the spiritual, which in turn cannot exist apart from the Divine-Humanity, or therefore from the history of salvation. Thus it is that God, humanity, culture, Church, the sense of history, and the spiritual come together and that the spiritual life finds its meaning in the eschatological dimension of this whole process. The spiritual life consists in seeing our daily life, this world, and this history in a new light with the help of the Holy Spirit.

Spiritual Fatherhood

A MAJESTIC PATH FOR PERSONAL WHOLENESS

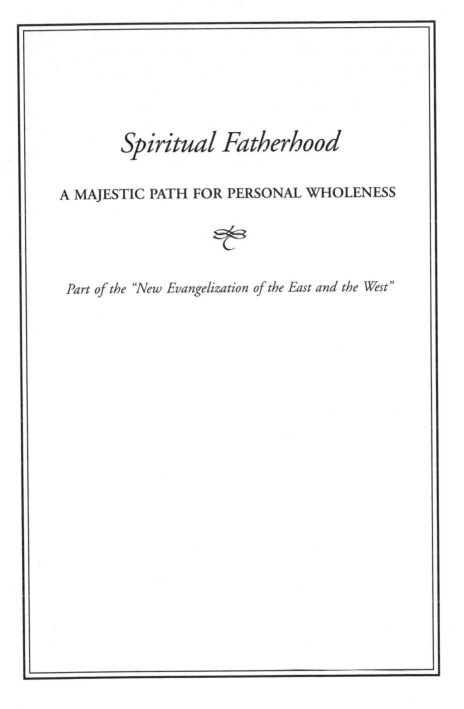

Part of the "New Evangelization of the East and the West"

1. The Context

We are living in an age that is witness to the sunset of modernity. We can already see some effects of the historical period that by now has concluded. It was a time of discovery of new concepts in science, a time of freedom, of the discovery of "autonomies." It was a time that saw the birth of a new religion of the mind, the time therefore of rationalism, of idealist enlightenment, as well as the time of technology and of human efforts to master the cosmos. Each of these realities has been carried out under the auspices of humanity and of humanism.[1] After the setting of these great promises, after the decline of this modern civilization that is so logical and well structured, when the great absolute, rational systems have been consumed, we find ourselves in an age that is still unformed, unsure, in which everything has been called into question, even though up until yesterday it represented an unquestionable certainty. This age has been called, as if to avoid any sort of prior definition, "postmodern."

This is not the place to wander into the many diverse analyses of contemporary society and culture. We only want to highlight some of the more outstanding characteristics of the state of the soul typical of this "postmodern" period. Postmodern persons do have a *state of soul* of which

---

1. Cf. Marecello Azevedo, "Inculturation and the Challenges of Modernity," *Inculturation* I (1982): 1-63; idem, "Challenges from Modern Culture," *Inculturation* II (1989): 63-77; Gianni Colzani, "Moderno, postmoderno e fede cristiana" (Modernity, Postmodernity, and the Christian Faith), *Aggiornamenti sociali* 12 (1990): 781.

Note from the author: In this article I will speak of "spiritual fatherhood" because that is what was written of by the great spiritual fathers. Regarding the spirituality of the female figure and spiritual maternity, I would recommend the various publications of Elisabeth Behr-Sigel; Mother Marie Skobtsova (1891-1945), who was a spiritual mother to and friend of many great European thinkers living in Paris and who wrote a series of very interesting essays; Pavel Evdokimov, *Women and the Salvation of the World* (Crestwood, NY: St. Vladimir's Seminary Press, 1994); M. Štremfelj, "Vivere la maternità spirituale oggi" (Living Spiritual Maternity Today), in Tomaš Špidlík, Sergio Rendina, et al., *In Colloquio: Alla scoperta dell paternità spirituale* (In Conversation: In Search of Spiritual Paternity) (Rome: Lipa, 1994), 223-247; and F. Morandi, "Dalla maternità alla maternità" (From Maternity to Maternity), in *In Colloquio*, 249-255.

contemporary art gives us clear evidence. The latest, great international expositions of contemporary painting and sculpture clearly highlight it, demonstrating in an impressive way that art unites people from different countries, cultures, and geographic areas — even different continents and political persuasions. Parallel to painting and sculpture, similar characteristics of this state of the soul can be identified in philosophy and in literature, in the theater, movies, music, and even in the empirical sciences.

Detachment from Objectivity

As a first and fundamental characteristic I would like to mention here a radical change in the understanding of what is objective reality and, therefore, in the ways of relating to objectivity.[2] Given that the objectively

2. Solov'ëv was already attentive to the gnoseological fundamentals of modern culture: "No real knowledge is exhausted in the data of our sensory experience (sensations) and in the forms of our rational thought (concepts)." The object "is only given to us as perceived and thought in these determined relationships, in other words, in its being relative" (Vladimir Solov'ëv, *Kritika otvlečënniych načal* [The Critique of Abstract Principles], in *Sobranie Sočinenii,* vol. 2 [Brussels: Foyer Oriental Chrétien, 1966]. Translated into Italian as *La critica dei principi astratti [1877-1880], in Sulla Divinoumanità e altri scritti* [Milan: Jaca, 1971], 197). The "unconditioned existence of the object would not be in any way accessible to me if between myself and the other there existed a perfect separation. In such a case, I could relate to them only externally and I would possess knowledge only of their relative being. Since in reality I have knowledge even of their unconditioned being, however, it follows that such a separation does not exist, and that the knower is in a certain way intimately linked with the one known, and a substantial union with them is found. This explains the immediate conviction with which we affirm the unconditioned existence of the other. According to this conviction, the knowing subject is *free,* unbound by facts of experience or by forms of pure thought — although affirming something that is not and cannot be either an empirical fact or a category of reason — and that is beyond the limits of both one and the other. According to this conviction our knowing subject does not act as an empirical sensing nor as a rational thinking but as absolute and free and thus even the object comes to be known in its absoluteness" (ibid., 200). "Rational thought taken in itself has no content and it cannot receive content *that corresponds to it,* that is, a total and true content, from external experience. Therefore, it must receive it from a positive and essential knowledge that is determined by faith and ideal contempla-

existing reality towards which the comprehension of the human intellect orients itself — culture, therefore — has changed, we are participating in a change in the definition that humanity has of itself that is also global. To explain better, if in the distant past humanity recognized divinity as objective existence, then this understanding was so absolute as to become overwhelming for human life.

We can therefore affirm with Solov'ëv that a totalitarian predominance of the divine, of the theological, was experienced.[3] With this key

---

tion. In other words, humans, as rational, receive their true and positive content from their mystical or divine element, and if we call philosophy the system of rational knowing, we must recognize that philosophy receives its content from religious or theological knowledge, understanding this as knowledge of all things in God or knowledge of the essential unitotality" (ibid., 212-213).

3. "In the field of knowledge the characteristic property of Western evolution is the consequent separating and exclusive atomizing of its three stages. First the division between sacred knowing, theology, and secular or natural knowing arose. During the Middle Ages the distinction between philosophy properly speaking and empirical science was not yet delineated within this secular knowing. Together they formed a single philosophy, the handmaid of theology, and only at the end of the Middle Ages (in the Renaissance) was it liberated from this service" (Vladimir Solov'ëv, *Filosofskie načala zel'nogo znanija* [The Philosophical Principles of Integral Knowledge], in *Sobranie Sočinenii*, vol. 1 [Brussels: Foyer Oriental Chrétien, 1966], translated into Italian as *I principi filosofici del sapere integrale,* in *Sulla Divinoumanità e altri scritti* [Milan: Jaca, 1971], 44). This consists of two passages of three moments in the evolution of the universal human organism. In the first state the levels "are undifferentiated and confused, so that each of them does not possess a truly distinct, autonomous being and exists only potentially. . . . This indifferentiation lies in the fact that the supreme or absolute stage swallows and hides all the others within itself, not permitting them to manifest themselves autonomously. In the second instance the inferior stages free themselves from the supreme power and tend toward absolute freedom. From the start they all rise up together against the supreme principle, renouncing it, but in order to acquire a complete development, each of them must affirm itself exclusively not only with respect to the supreme principle, but also against all the others. It must also renounce these others. Thus, in the common struggle of the inferior elements against the supreme stage, an internal struggle within the inferior stages themselves necessarily derives as well. After this process, however, the supreme stage rises up, establishes itself as such, acquires freedom, and thus creates the conditions for a new unity" (ibid., 35-36). In fact, for "achieving the supreme, common goal of knowledge, a goal determined by theology, . . . this in turn should renounce the illicit pretext of regulating the instruments

we can better understand the age from the Renaissance on when humanity discovered the possibility of separating itself from this divine totality, affirming its self-autonomy, and thus affirming the human in its independence from the religious: "The person who has left behind every form of minority is a person that affirms the self subjectively in a logic of immanence and in a dynamic of refusing the Christian faith and its influence."[4] However, this "liberation of human energies" does not occur without making them superficial, without losing the connection with that spiritual depth to which they were joined and intimately bound.[5]

This person is "taken in . . . isolation and external, superficial reality"[6] having "proclaimed the self, in this false position, the sole divinity as well as an insignificant atom."[7] Humanity cannot exist, cannot reason except by orienting itself toward a fixed, objective reference point. Precisely because of this necessity, these reference points remain even into the modern age, but time and time again they are changed according to what is considered the most "objective" reality. "But where can we find this absolute content of life and knowledge?"[8] In postmodernism, "once this value has dissolved, it is reality itself that loses its meaning: in the postmodern experience, reality no longer has the solid, objective meaning that it held for humanity in the past."[9] Thus there was a time that saw the predominance of thought, of the idea understood in its abstractness as eternal, truly objective, and universal. It was a time, therefore, when, within the sphere of philosophy, there occurred an orientation of everything toward objectivity. Then there was a time of the predomi-

---

of philosophical cognition, of limiting scientific matter, and of interfering in their respective spheres as medieval theology had done. Only a theology that has an autonomous philosophy and science behind it can transform itself together with these into a free theosophy, because the one which gives freedom to others is the only free one" (ibid., 51).

4. Colzani, "Moderno, postmoderno e fede cristiana," 781-782.

5. Nikolai Berdiaev, *Smysl istorii* (Paris: YMCA Press, 1948). Translated into English as *The Meaning of History*, tr. George Reavey (London: G. Bles, 1936), 130-131.

6. Solov'ëv, *I principi filosofici del sapere integrale*, 48.

7. Ibid.

8. Ibid., 49.

9. Gianni Vattimo, "Il museo e l'esperienza dell'arte nella postmodernità" (The Museum and the Experience of Art in Postmodernity), *Rivista di estetica* 37 (1991): 4.

nance of nature and the empirical. "Scientific" objectivity, an application of conceptual structures to natural laws, prevailed. Thus empirical science, according to Cartesian-Newtonian paradigms, became the code for the affirmation of the objective, of the undisputed, and therefore of the universal.[10]

Then came sociology's turn. It was focused on as a way to understand what was most objective for humanity and what conditioned it the most. The most surprising thing is that at the close of this process, which evolved along the arc of modernity, humanity concentrated on itself, becoming the only real objective, the subject understood above all as sensation of itself, as a state of the soul, often as a perception of the feeling of self or even as a sensorial sensation.[11] If modernity began with the affirmation of logic and systematic rationalism that claimed to be universal, it ends with the revenge of subjectivism or individualism, in any case, with the revenge of a culture of self-assertion. There is an explosion of styles in art, but they lack any communicative force, any communitarian content.[12]

Art, the queen of a language that tended towards universal communication, winds up as the spent, lamenting song of many separate individuals who continually look only upon and speak only to themselves. Art became a sob, the vomit of what the individual had suffered in modern society. Exhibits have become the "confessional" of what happened

10. On "progress" and "development" as magical words in the modern era, cf. Italo Vaccarini, "La condizione 'postmoderna': Una sfida per la cultura cristiana" (The "Postmodern" Condition: A Challenge for Christian Culture), *Aggiornamenti sociali* 12 (1990): 127; Gianni Vattimo, "Il museo e l'esperienza dell'arte nella postmodernità," 4; and Guglielmo Forni, *Reflessioni sull'idea di modernità* (Reflections on the Idea of Modernity) (Genoa: Marietti, 1992), 44-56.

11. "Feeling themselves the center of reality because all must converge upon them can easily lead to the temptation to consider the world as real only in so far as it is perceptible. Giving in to this temptation, even sensorial reality is lost, only their own subjective selves remain as experience of reality. All the rest, the external world and other people, scarcely seems real, becoming pure appearance, even if beautiful and fascinating" (Heinrich Pfeiffer, "Le dimensioni dell'arte" [The Dimensions of Art], *Nuova Umanità* 1 [1979]: 94-95).

12. Cf. Alberto Boatto, "I pop artists: Gli ultimi 'peintres de la vie moderne'" (Pop Artists: The Last "Painters of the Modern Way"), in *Arte Americana* (Milan: Fabbri, 1992), 240.

within persons no longer able to go out of themselves.[13] A superficial generalization of consumerism has led the desire to be unique, original, unmistakable to exasperation. This is why every artist has invented new forms, new styles, without a code for understanding, without communication.[14] The same thing happened in the fields of philosophy and science. If a sole logic dominated for a long time, all at once we realized that we are living in a pluralism of logics, and what one science developed within its area of expertise began to contradict other sciences.

The culture that developed "is in its deepest essence eclectic and contradictory; it is an analytically fractional culture composed of contradictory elements each of which ceaselessly strives for complete independence."[15] Every field of knowledge affirms it own truth and objectivity, up to a dangerous atomism in which the threat of the spiritual, psychological, and physical destruction of humanity has become completely real. "The selfish, singular interest, the casual fact, the limited particular, atomism in life, science, and art, is the last word of Western civilization. . . . This civilization elaborated particular forms and material exteriors for life but did not give to humanity the interior content of life itself. After having highlighted certain, particular elements, it brought them to the greatest level of development, as much as possible in their separation, but left them without an organic connection and therefore deprived of a living spirit making all this richness dead capital."[16]

Summarizing this first characteristic, we can affirm that postmodern

13. Cf. Colzani, "Moderno, postmoderno e fede cristiana," 789.

14. Cf. Pavel Florenskij, *Obratnaja perspektiva* (Reverse Perspective), in *Izbranye trudy po estetike* (Paris, 1985), 165-166, translated into Italian as *La prospettiva rovesciata e altri scritti* (Rome: Casa del Libro, 1983), 126. "If all people feel, individually, as if they are at the center of reality, then communication between them becomes difficult. Each sees only one aspect of things and tries to judge the rest from this aspect, trying to make his or her own point of view hold firm over everyone else's. All values become subjective and relative; everyone can establish individually what art is. It is sufficient that an individual's artistic self-affirmation find a wide following in society to make his or her works valuable as works of art" (Pfeiffer, "Le dimensioni dell'arte," 95).

15. Pavel Florenskij, *Ikonostasis,* tr. Donald Sheehan and Olga Andrejev (Crestwood, NY: St. Vladimir's Seminary Press, 1996), 147.

16. Solov'ëv, *I principi filosifici del sapere integrale,* 48.

humanity finds itself detached from the unquestionably existent objectivity, which is life itself. Separated thus from life, we find ourselves imprisoned in many intellectual, sociological, scientific, political, and cultural systems and structures, all however without breath or direction, without life-giving nourishment. In the desperate search for life, we are oriented towards the psyche, concentrating on what it feels and proclaims to be most urgent, pressing, and objective on the horizon. We focus on what is felt, on what is believed, without any real distinction between the sensation, the feeling, or the thought. We are in the age of psychologism.[17]

The Need for Consolation

Another characteristic easily deducible from the previous one is that we are in an age of searching for consolations. If the modern age promised individual happiness based on economic well-being, today we are witnesses of the disappointment provoked by this false expectation. We live in a society that is jam-packed with things, but people are disappointed because they are not happy. Rather, the more common feeling is boredom.[18] Given that modern society, rationalist and technocratic as it is, has given life to a reified culture, a culture of things, such that the entire part that is most typically human, the relational dimension, the dimension of love, has become handicapped, deprived of realization.

Since happiness, therefore, belongs strictly to this sphere, we witness

17. Cf. Christopher Lasch, *The Culture of Narcissism: American Life in an Age of Diminishing Expectations* (New York: Norton, 1979).

18. "Those who do not admit of any reality, other than the one visible in itself of the external world, must renounce any ideal content of life and any true knowledge or art whatsoever. In such a case nothing remains for a person except the inferior animal life in which happiness, if it occurs, is always an illusion. On the other hand, the tendency to the superior life and the awareness of one's dissatisfaction remain, thus the natural conclusion is that life is a game that is not worth anything and the absolute void appears as the desired end of the individual and the whole of society" (Solov'ëv, *I principi filosofici del sapere integrale*, 49).

the strange phenomenon of people who are satisfied by specific things that they have acquired but who are unhappy. They therefore try to satisfy that dimension that has been denied true life. They no longer look to a consolation derived only from things, from having, but together with consumerist enjoyment they look for satisfaction in the sphere of relationships and in everything typical of it, most of all in the psychological and spiritual spheres. Thus an entire relational art of the awakening awareness of relationships is invented, which in effect, however, remains a fiction, a conviction of being in a more than real relationship that surpasses the boundaries of one's very self, an essential recognition of and an orientation of the energies of one's life toward the other.

Beyond all psychological exercises and mental attentions, there is also evidence of a wide market of the para-religious, the clear sign of which is the spread of sects. A common denominator of all these proposals is the strong emphasis on consolation and self-realization. We cannot deny that, in spite of this, humanity is extremely susceptible and incapable of true relationship that takes the objectivity of the other into account, recognizing it as such.

A Handicap to Knowing God

This tragedy of relationships — we can call it that — lived at the sunset of the modern era, has profound and disturbing consequences. If God is Love, that is, absolute connectedness, then he is not knowable in a purely abstract or conceptual manner or in any other way that is distanced from relating to him. According to ancient patristic tradition, God is known by relating to him in a loving relationship and is experienced in such complete encounter that it does not exclude any human dimension but rather involves the entire human.[19]

---

19. Cf. "Connaître" in Xavier Leon-Dufour, *Vocabulaire de théologie biblique* (Dictionary of Biblical Theology) (Paris: Cerf, 1971), 199-204. See also Pavel Evdokimov, *La connaissance de Dieu selon la tradition orientale* (The Knowledge of God in the Eastern Tradition) (Paris: Desclée de Brouwer, 1988).

If, however, we live in a reified society, in a culture characterized by subjectivist rationalism, if, moreover, there practically does not exist any-one who has a positive experience of interpersonal relationships with his or her family, it is legitimate to ask: How is it possible to know God today if he reveals himself in relationships?

Someone might object, saying that God can also be known through na-ture and in creation. However, even on that subject, at the end of the histor-ical period that has seen the predominance of a culture of the technological warping of creation, an industrialized, informatic, and urban culture, there are entire generations who have never lived a single, authentic cosmic expe-rience. Today, people often discover only at the end of a dramatic and tragic journey filled with deceptions and disappointments the benevolence and the tenderness of God who encounters them in the light.

The Shattering of the Lived Experience

At the end of the modern era, the fact that God is far from thought or, at least, that we have become accustomed to living as if he did not exist, is responsible for the experience of the fractured personality.[20] We see how people are continuously faced with antinomies that are ever more irrecon-cilable with their personal experiences and with their lives. We continu-ally find ourselves behaving differently according to the different contexts in which we have to live. The individual life falls prey to the diverse de-sires that correspond to the diverse criteria that must be overcome one by one as they arrive. Everything becomes a fleeting, occasional moment, and the affirmation of self is concentrated in a precise moment that must necessarily be followed by another in order to conquer and overcome the ever more frequent enemies: boredom, monotony, and forgetfulness.

20. "Only when the people's will and intellect enter into communion with the eter-nal and true being will all the forms and particular elements of life and knowledge acquire a positive meaning and value and be all the instruments necessary for or mediative of one, complete life. Their contradiction and enmity based on each one's exclusive self affirma-tion will necessarily disappear as soon as all together freely submit to the principle and central totality" (Solov'ëv, *I principi filosofici del sapere integrale*, 50).

Sin and Memory

Things that we have experienced, done, or undergone, strangely enough, beyond every social and ethical condition, begin to weigh heavily, to come often to mind, and to resurface in consciousness. The memory of someone distanced from the God of Love, from the God of Mercy, can be compared to the memory of a computer. It is a fossilized memory that, therefore, needs to be erased in order to free it. In this way, memory becomes a curse because it is capable of pursuing someone who is trying everything in his or her power to pacify it.

More and more, many paths of psychoanalysis, of coming to awareness, and even more banal ways arise to help someone forget. People today make more of an effort to forget than to remember. A tormented memory, disturbed by unaccepted experiences, always increases conflict at the personal as well as the interpersonal level. A memory that is not taken care of destroys one's relationship with self, with the environment, with history, and above all, with the future. A bad memory causes the death of creativity.

Facile judgments and prejudices come from a memory that is not healed. A prejudice is not something abstract but is rooted in a distancing derived from a negative experience that has never been accepted. Prejudice easily condemns the mind, in itself already so attuned to evil and inclined to doubt, suspicion, and curiosity for the negative. In the age of mass media — the true power of the contemporary age — we must realize that we are living with an overwhelming amount of information about evil.

New Closures

Evil is, on the one hand, quite fascinating for our minds and imaginations. On the other, it demands justice, the indicting of the guilty, and reparation for the evil committed. Since evil, for many throughout the world, is identified with the fear of losing something already acquired, the bad guy is the one who presents himself as a threat. This is a plausible explanation for the new nationalisms that are developing in Europe under two different aspects.

In the West, we find a nationalism that wants at all cost to guard and maintain what the modern era has achieved and that feels menaced by every eventual change that might represent a passage from better to worse. In the East instead, a nationalism is developing with the characteristic of forcefully demanding what was denied or suppressed for decades by imposed collectivism and internationalism. Thus we are faced with a new hardening of relationships where the other no longer represents a stimulus, but rather is a danger.

Even pluralism, so highly extolled by the modern era, no longer receives credit because different opinions now represent a disturbance, a threat. One opts, therefore, for indifference. In this culture characterized by individualistic closures, in this chaos of subjectivism where everything is relative and not even human life represents an indisputable value, the voices of some young thinkers calling for order, a strong hand, for discipline in thinking and acting, and so on, are heard more and more often.

We are witnesses of nostalgia for systems and regimes that ten years ago seemed buried forever. We also witness ever more frequent calls for laws and discipline. Yet the modern age has acquired some values that are impossible to abandon. This means bringing them back to life and personalizing them in a faith that envelops things and makes them immortal.

2. Some Indispensable Characteristics of the Spiritual Father

In the context of contemporary Europe, the Church desires to proclaim Christ with a new strength and conviction. Beginning from a vital witness, she wants to promote a new evangelization. It is along this path that the fatherly/motherly spirituality, transmitted to us by the Church from the earliest times, is located. This is not the place to argue for the importance of this way of proclamation and formation; it is simply one of many ways. I would, however, like to point out that without spiritual fatherhood/motherhood, the new evangelization will not have the impact and depth necessary to truly accomplish its mission in Europe that by now is profoundly de-Christianized. Let us now try to highlight some salient traits of spiritual fatherhood that, mindful of the contemporary cultural and spiritual situation, will show how much the contribution of this art can mean today.

When I speak of spiritual fatherhood, I refer to that tradition that has been understood as a gift of the Holy Spirit, as an exceptional charisma, and that had an extraordinary development in ancient monasticism.[21] After many centuries, through the *starets* of the Russian Church, it reflourished as a true art and source of the rebirth of the faith and the Church, which were hard tried by compromises with the world's powers and mentality.

In the West, it was transformed more into a ministry and called "spiritual direction." It should also be said that there was no lack of hardships and that it suffered many deviations, above all in formative institutions such as seminaries, novitiates, and associations. After Vatican II, under the influence of more personalistic directions that underlined the Christian vocation, spiritual fatherhood was again understood as a vocation as well, and was therefore linked to the Christian vocation.

It is clear that this does not mean a weakening of the vocation of the spiritual father properly speaking. Rather, we can note a reflourishing of spiritual fatherhood understood once again in a synthetic way, where at the center is found a charism, a gift, enriched by tradition, knowledge, and reflection on experience. It is not easy, however, to find a good spiritual father. Further, given that the request is so great, we can even expect many mistakes in this area, given that error, in itself, already accompanies every human activity.

Because such mistakes are personal, however, it is necessary to do everything possible to avoid them. It seems important to me, therefore, to highlight some characteristics that sketch out the figures of the spiritual father and mother. I choose those indispensable characteristics that are

21. Cf. Irenée Hausherr, *Spiritual Direction in the Early Christian East* (Kalamazoo, MI: Cistercian Publications, 1990). As already mentioned, where "fatherhood/spiritual father" is spoken of, the reference to the reality of spiritual fatherhood/motherhood should always be made.

possible and that can represent for us the guarantee of a proper exercise of spiritual accompaniment today.

a. A Spiritual Father Is a Person Filled with the Holy Spirit

A spiritual father is one who, in the creative power of the Holy Spirit, generates persons for God. He is one by means of whom what is said after the *Sanctus* in the Fourth Eucharistic Prayer is accomplished: "so that we might live no longer for ourselves but for him who died and rose for us." The spiritual father carries this charism of generation and so has a mission that is closely linked to life. "The meaning of true fatherhood is . . . *giving one's life.*"[22]

b. A Spiritual Father Is a Person Who Knows the Heart

The Holy Spirit, who searches the depths of God and gives life to the human spirit, is the One who discloses hearts to the spiritual father.[23] This knowledge of the other is not something miraculous or a quality characteristic of clairvoyants, an oddity, but rather is a fruit of the Holy Spirit developed in a second moment through the reflection that a spiri-

22. Gabriel Bunge, *Geistliche Vaterschaft: Christliche Gnosis bei Evagrios Pontikos* (Spiritual Fatherhood: Christian Gnosis according to Evagrius Ponticus) (Regensburg: Pustet, 1988), 15.

23. "'The first thought that comes to me I take as coming from God, and I speak without knowing what is occurring in the soul of the person I am speaking with but knowing that it is the will of God and that it is for the person's good. At times, trusting my reason, I respond, thinking it were something easy. In these cases, however, I err. As the iron is shaped at the anvil so I entrust my will to God. I act as he wills, not possessing a will of my own.' But Father Anthony responded that he saw the person's soul like a face in a mirror thanks to the purity of the heart. Father Seraphim put his right hand on the mouth of the hegumen. 'No, my joy, you must not speak like that. The human heart is open to God alone. If one draws near to another, one sees how deep the heart of the other is' (Ps. 64:7)" (Séraphim of Sarov, *Sa vie, Entretien avec Motovilov et Instructions spirituelles* [His Life, Interview with Motovilov and Spiritual Instructions], tr. Irina Goraïnoff [Paris: Desclée de Brouwer, 1995], 61).

tual father makes of his own experience and the experience related to him by others. In effect, knowledge of the heart is nothing other than an intuition of love toward the person, toward the other, just as towards oneself.[24]

This very specific characteristic of the knowledge of the heart is one of the fundamental elements that guarantees a healthy spiritual fatherhood because it is the radical affirmation of love[25] as a cognitive principle. Love as a cognitive principle belongs to interpersonal knowledge. The more I love, the more I know.[26]

It is only on this principle that the human person is cared for on the truly personal level, not letting the person fall to the level of an object, relating to him or her with a typically empirical or analytical knowledge. This is not a mysticism of the knowledge of the other but a total, careful, perceptive knowledge that can even be analytical, but with the fundamental characteristic that all of these data are imbued with love, read with the eyes of love, from which comes the comprehension of the other.

24. "To be in love with another's personality is to perceive the identity and unity underlying its perpetual change and division; it is to perceive its nobility even in the midst of utter degradation. Love is the means by which the obscurity of the objective world is illuminated and the heart of existence is penetrated, so that the Thou may displace and, finally, annihilate the object" (Nikolai Berdiaev, *Ja i mir* [Paris: YMCA Press, 1934], translated into English as *Solitude and Society*, tr. George Reavey [New York: Charles Scribner's Sons, 1939], 196). "This awareness [of the personality] is founded upon love as the intuition of the personality. We should endeavor to exercise this intuition about our own selves as well as about others. . . . Thus the development of the personality implies sacrifice and renunciation, the ultimate triumph over egocentrism, but never self-hate" (ibid., 197).

25. "Recognizing in love the truth of another, not abstractly, but essentially, transferring in deed the center of our life beyond the limits of our empirical personality, we by so doing reveal and realize our own real truth, our own absolute significance, which consists just in our capacity to transcend the borders of our factual phenomenal being, in our capacity to live not only in ourselves, but also in another" (Vladimir Solov'ëv, *Smysl ljubvi*, in *Sobranie Sočinenii*, vol. 7 [Brussels: Foyer Oriental Chrétien, 1966], translated into English as *The Meaning of Love*, tr. Thomas R. Beyer Jr. [Hudson, NY: Lindisfarne Press, 1985], 45).

26. Cf. Origen, *The Song of Songs: Commentary and Homilies*, tr. R. P. Lawson (Westminster, MD: Newman Press, 1957).

c. A Spiritual Father Is a Person of Discernment

From the two preceding characteristics it is easy to arrive at the third, the capacity to discern which thoughts and feelings God speaks through that are oriented towards him and which ones constitute a deception, which is often disguised behind the appearance of goodness.[27] The spiritual father, therefore, is a master at creating an appointment between a person and God, given that he knows well the behaviors of both one as well as the Other when they are approaching one another. It is spiritual sobriety, emotional and rational, that accompanies discernment and constitutes a typical characteristic of it. This prevents a spiritual father from invading the intimate and entirely personal areas of the other. On the other hand, it supplies the spiritual father with objective elements for transmitting the art of discerning to the other who thus becomes a mature Christian.

d. A Spiritual Father Is One Who Teaches and Adheres to Tradition

A spiritual father does not act alone, boasting of his charism and relying only on his own intuitions. In fact, spiritual fathers are normally recognized by the fact that, with profound humility, they search for connections with the Tradition of the great spiritual masters and succeed in showing others that their experience is not something isolated but is woven into the fabric of many past spiritual relationships. This is why a spiritual father is also a person of study, of reflection, with a certain gift for words that allows him to teach.[28]

27. "The charism of *diorasis* remained therefore a sign of the Spirit and was composed of two main elements: a knowledge of the mysteries of God (theology) and an understanding of the secrets of the heart *(cardiognosis)*. It was a spiritual perspicuity that saw through the flesh, through time, and through space *(proorasis)*" (Tomaš Špidlík, *The Spirituality of the Christian East: A Systematic Handbook,* tr. Anthony P. Gythiel [Kalamazoo, MI: Cistercian Publications, 1986], 77).

28. St. Basil called this the *diakonia tou logou,* the service of the word (*Homélies sur l'Hexaéméron* (Homilies on the Hexaemeron), ed. Stanislas Giet, SC 26bis [Paris: Cerf, 1968], 388). "Abba, give us a word," the apothegms often repeat.

A spiritual father must be able to transmit the vital spark of the saints of the past to people today, often a problematic task. When a spiritual father speaks, many of his friends from the distant past become so vividly present in his words that it is as if they were his contemporaries. The entire Church resounds in a spiritual father. For this reason, he cannot help but bring attention to the community, to ecclesiality.[29] This, above all, is the radical difference between a *guru* and a spiritual father.

Besides which, the importance of a certain knowledge of modern sciences and psychology should not be forgotten; just the opposite, it must be well noted. I do not mean to say that psychology "saves"; nevertheless, it is a clear aid to the salvation that the Spirit works in people. Given that the spiritual life unfolds in this continuous, reciprocal passage from the divine to the human — thus also to the psychological and the sensorial — many laws of the reactions in such spheres are precisely illuminated by psychology, which helps us to understand how to be open to a more complete and serene adhesion to God, from whom comes every salvation and every gift of life.

When I speak of "psychology" I am referring to that talent of a natural psychological intelligence that is developed in perfect harmony with the deeper examination of psychology as a science. I would, however, be cautious with regard to those spiritual fathers who are first and foremost psychologists — who mainly interpret everything on the basis of the study of psychology, psychotherapy, psychoanalysis, or depth psychology — and only add some spiritual "connotations" to this basic interpretation because they, sometimes, happen to also be priests or religious.

e. A Spiritual Father Is One Who Serves God and Others

A spiritual father is not oriented toward himself, to his doctrine or wisdom, but has an attitude of submission to God. He acts according to divine will and is directed toward those whom God wants to reach. A true

---

29. Tomaš Špidlík, "La direzione spirituale nell'Oriente cristiano" (Spiritual Direction in the Christian East), *Vita consacrata* 16 (1980): 503-514, 573-585.

spiritual father rejoices in finishing his service. After having led people to the art of discernment, after having created this appointment between the person and God, his role decreases. When the spiritual children succeed in seeing themselves with the love of God, the spiritual father can withdraw. He accompanies them to the threshold of the Father.

This is clearly seen in the calling of Samuel. When Samuel hears that someone is calling him, he runs to the father, his own "polar star." His heart, his interior world, is "structured" to the image of relationship. Having a father means not being lost, having coordinates for the search, knowing to whom to turn. After the third call, Samuel comes to Eli who refers him to the true Father in whom the foundation of every fatherhood is found.

This is why there is no true fatherhood that does not lead to its foundation, the Father of Jesus Christ. In that moment, old Eli had not "accomplished" his own mission but had lived it in its fullness because he had educated the young man in the knowledge that is fulfilled in relationship, had trained him to listen for God who reveals himself personally, through relationships.

f. A Spiritual Father Prays with Others and for Others

The spiritual father continually accompanies persons entrusted to him in prayer. He sustains them in prayer, joining his heart to them, praying with them, invoking grace and mercy for them. This is why a spiritual father must accept as many persons for direction as he can commend to the Father in the Holy Spirit.

g. A Spiritual Father Is Indicated by Others

A spiritual father does not place himself on display or advertise himself. A spiritual father is discovered following a path that is well-beaten because so many people have already traveled it to get to him. A spiritual father is recognized by the threshold that is well-worn with the many steps that crossed it seeking wisdom. However, all of this is only one aspect of the criteria. It must be completed with another: the lives of the ones who come seeking guidance. In fact, the witness of the spiritual children's lived experience is the guarantee that a spiritual father is truly such.

We hear the voice of a spiritual father and we hope to be able to be received by him. Those who are called to be spiritual fathers, or whom life itself has placed in this position, must not oppress themselves with perfectionism, that is, they must not become moralistic with themselves. The important thing is that, even if they possess little of what was mentioned above, they at least have a small part of these characteristics and that their development moves within these coordinates.

3. The Work of a Spiritual Father

The Interpersonal Relationship with a Spiritual Father as a Place of the Knowledge of God

A spiritual father is one with whom an experience of healthy relationship is lived out. In fact, a relationship with a spiritual father is an area in which the person — especially today when we are so often wounded in the area of relationships — can live a true, authentic experience of what is spiritually an "interpersonal relationship."[30]

30. *Giving one's life* "means offering another the space to freely be oneself. The sense of true 'filiation' — certainly, not a less important aspect — is the free welcoming of oneself as *being-in-relationship.* 'Father' and 'son' in the field of spirituality, regardless of the physical sex or age of the persons in question, are metaphors that express a *relationship.* Tradition, therefore, does not only know spiritual 'fathers,' but also spiritual 'mothers.' Now, as the same 'father-son' image is also applied to the divine persons of the Holy Trinity, what is at stake is evident. Whoever does not experience true fatherhood and true filiation in spirituality also runs the risk of not having a true personal experience of God. Spiritual fatherhood means nothing less than the experience of *overcoming* one's own individuality in the *encounter* with a 'you' who bears the ancient name of 'father,' because in such an overcoming he becomes 'the one who generates' his being-person. In an absolute sense, this experience of becoming-person is uniquely realized in the encounter with the 'you' of God, whom we, thanks to the Son, in the Holy Spirit, can call 'Abba, Father!'" (Bunge, *Geistliche Vaterschaft,* 18).

When I use the term "spiritual" I mean by it everything that communicates God, that speaks of God, that narrates his story, that leads back to him, that orients life toward God.[31] To sum up, "spiritual" is what I call that process by means of which a person begins to open up, to see beyond the confines of the self, everything that orients a person toward the other, that allows the person to live the indispensable dimension of religiosity.[32]

By "religiosity" I mean that religious principle that for Solov'ëv is the recognition of the unconditioned existence of the other.[33] A spiritual father, in relationship, creates the possibility of a spiritual experience of relationship itself for the other. The person should experience that the spiritual father recognizes him or her completely, considers that person in an absolute way, that the true relationship is going out of the self and recognizing the epicenter in the other.[34]

Even for a spiritual father this is an experience of God, of his love, with whose strength he is able to relate to others in a free and disinterested way. The other lives this relationship as an authentic experience of love because he or she feels recognized, considered in the mystery of being a person, not forced, or manipulated, or seen indifferently.

This sphere of relationship will be a "burning bush" for the person. The presence of God, for whoever goes to a spiritual father, will initially still be an a-categorical experience. Little by little, however, it will arouse

31. Špidlík, *The Spirituality of the Christian East*, 29-30.

32. Cf. Marko I. Rupnik, "La vita spirituale" (Spiritual Life), in Tomaš Špidlík, Maria Campitalli, et al., *Lezioni sulla Divinoumanità* (Rome: Lipa, 1995), 279-333.

33. "Faith in the strict sense of the term is the affirmation of an absolute existence . . . an unconditioned existence. This absoluteness applies equally to all that exists in so far as it is" (Solov'ëv, *La critica dei principi astratti*, 203). Solov'ëv makes the same affirmation regarding love as well as faith: "Love . . . is the transfer of all our interest in life from ourselves to another, as the shifting of the very center of our personal lives" (Solov'ëv, *The Meaning of Love*, 51).

34. "The life of the personality is most intimately associated with love, without which there is no self-fulfillment, no overcoming of isolation, no communion. Love in its turn postulates the personality: It is the relationship of one personality to another, the means of freeing the personality from the prison of self and of allowing it to identify itself with another personality — the art by which it receives eternal acknowledgment and confirmation" (Berdiaev, *Solitude and Society*, 195).

the respect necessary to lift the intellect away from things and make it capable of focusing on the other, as happened with Moses who drew near to the bush to see what it was and then found himself speaking with a "You." He found himself having to seriously take God, who began to make himself known, into consideration.

The relationship with the spiritual father is precisely the location, the "Emmaus," in which, conversing, breaking the bread, a person will one day recognize Christ. Where there is love, God is there. Given that God is Love,[35] absolute relation, interpersonal relationship is precisely the privileged place of the knowledge of God, that is, of his revelation. According to the words of Kallistos Kataphygiotes: "The greatest thing that takes place between God and the soul is loving and being loved."[36]

Witness of Mercy

A spiritual father should, with his presence filled with the Spirit and with a spiritual gaze, witness to the gaze of Christ, that gaze that accompanied Peter for three years of walking together and that Peter, in the courtyard of the High Priest, finally grasped in its fullness. A spiritual father should communicate this immensely merciful gaze.[37]

One day I was speaking to a student in my office where a large painting of the face of Christ that I had just finished was sitting on an easel. It was a period in which I was drawing near to a Byzantine interpretation of the figure of Christ, therefore it was a luminous face, suffering but majestic, with two large compassionate eyes. The two of us were seated on either side of the easel.

35. Of the immense bibliography that could be cited on the topic of this "love of reciprocity" that constitutes the bond of the Trinity, we limit ourselves to noting Sergius Bulgakov, *Utešitel'* (Paris: YMCA Press, 1936), translated into Italian as *Il Paraclito* (The Paraclete) (Bologna: Dehoniane, 1971), 142, and G. M. Zanghì, *Dio che è Amore* (God That Is Love) (Rome: Città Nuova, 1991), 115.

36. *De vita contemplativa* (On the Contemplative Life), PG 147.860.

37. "On Repentance," in Archimandrite Sophrony (Sakharov), *St. Silouan the Athonite,* tr. Rosemary Edmonds (Crestwood, NY: St. Vladimir's Seminary Press, 1999), 345-352.

I asked the student, "According to you, at whom is Christ looking?"

"He is looking at me."

Then I asked him to get up and to continue looking at Christ and, step by step, slowly, to come over to my side. I asked him again, "Now you are alone, your head is full of bad thoughts, violent thoughts. And Christ?"

"He is looking at me," he responded.

At the next step I said to him, "You are with your friends, drunk, on a Saturday night. And Christ?"

"He is looking at me," he said again.

Still another step and I asked him, "Now you are with your fiancée, living sexually in the way you have spoken to me about, which disturbs your memory. And Christ?"

"He is looking at me with the same mercy."

When he was almost at my side, I said, "And now you are in church, at Mass, and you are reading the readings. And Christ?"

"He is looking at me with great compassion."

"So," I told him, "when you feel Christ's compassionate and merciful gaze upon you in all of the circumstances of your life, you will be a truly spiritual person, you will be entirely whole again, at what we can call interior peace, a serenity of the soul, a happiness in life. When you discover yourself in his merciful gaze and feel his Love enveloping you like a balm, all of the situations in your life that we have talked about will be changed. A person changes because of the love that fills the heart. One sins because of a lack of love, or rather, because one does not accept the Love that awaits in the heart."

A spiritual father judges the sins, not the sinner, and both on his face and in their relationship a person should find a rapport characterized by a limitless, untiring welcome.

Mediator

It is useless to think that a spiritual father might, psychologically, have enough energy to be able to tirelessly accommodate everyone, each and every crisis, to pick up all the pieces. A spiritual father is simply a mediator. In himself, oriented toward the Father, he seeks to communicate what he contemplates within to the person before him. The more he learns to see with the eyes of the loving Father, the more he is a spiritual father for himself and others.

Fidelity as an Experience of the Objectivity of Relationships

Fidelity is the most objective accomplishment of interpersonal relationships. This is why, already in the Old Testament, God formed his people through the Covenant. Therefore, Christ with the new and eternal Covenant represents the greatest fullness of love imaginable. The more mature and purified a love is, the more faithful it is.[38] Without fidelity it cannot be called love. Because a spiritual father has experienced the fidelity of the Father's mercy, even to the point of sacrifice, he also becomes faithfulness for the spiritual children who entrust themselves to him.

Given that today we note many difficulties in creating true relationships,[39] it is precisely by means of fidelity that a spiritual father represents that relational objectivity, which the other person must take into account. That is why a spiritual father, in the fidelity that can only exist in love, can tell the other person even those things that they might not want to hear or that might seem insensitive at a time when they would expect enthusiasm or approval. This is the way a spiritual father introduces them to the art of accepting the objectivity of the other.

38. It is this penetration of love-faith (cf. note 33) that makes the "impenetrability of time" surpass reality. This "impenetrability of time" consists of the fact that "every successive moment of existence does not preserve the preceding one within itself, but excludes it or dislodges it from existence, so that each new thing in the sphere of matter originates at the expense of, or to the detriment of, what preceded it" (Solov'ëv, *The Meaning of Love*, 106).

39. In an age when everything is reversible and the refusal of every continuity reigns, in an age when we experience human relations that are completely scarred as well as the incapacity to make definitive choices, we nevertheless witness many symptoms of a fidelity that has become impossible but at the same time yearned for. See for example *La messa è finita* (The Mass is Ended), the film by Nanni Moretti that has been defined as "a great canticle of fidelity": M. Nicoletti, "La città, un prete e la ricerca della fedeltà" (The City, a Priest, and the Search for Fidelity), *Il Margine* 1 (1986): 29-33.

It is that inevitable step towards maturity, which goes beyond mere pleasantries and begins the work of taking on objectivity in life. This attitude, however, is a sure path only if it is rooted in the Redeemer whom the spiritual father contemplates in his heart.

Entrusting the Lives of Others to God

Thanks to this continuous inner contemplation, thanks to an unceasing openness to the Spirit of the Father, a spiritual father, as mediator, entrusts and communicates what he sees, hears, and knows to the merciful Father. Given that the person who comes to him is not yet able to entrust his or her own life to God — and consequently is experiencing a dispersion and a loss of life that keeps many experiences closed, isolated, and destined to the definite forgetting that is death — a spiritual father, while listening to this person, entrusts this recounting to God in his own heart through the power of the Holy Spirit.

Spiritual fatherhood is actually based on our faith in the presence of the Holy Spirit, in his indwelling in a person, and in his efficacy in moving creation and humanity, through Christ, to the Father. It is the spiritual father, then, who points out the inner connections between various experiences, connections that appear immediately when one's lived experiences are opened up to God.[40] With the art of discernment he assists persons in deciphering the language God uses with them and in discovering God's word for them in the events of their life.

In this way a person's life becomes more and more entrusted to God,

---

40. This does not consist in developing the single elements of life, "but of vivifying and spiritualizing the elements that are adversarial and dead in their enmity, of giving them an absolute general content, and with this of freeing them from exclusivist self-affirmations and mutual negation" (Solov'ëv, *I principi filosofici del sapere integrale*, 49). This principle is found "in the absolute divine world that is infinitely more real and richer than this world of superficial, apparent phenomena. This admission is at the same time more natural in that humanity, by its eternal principle, belongs to that divine, transcendent world and has maintained with it, in the superior levels of its life and its knowing, a connection that is not just substantial but also actual." Ibid.

becomes *"hidden with Christ in God"* (Col. 3:3). Slowly, with the help of the spiritual father, this person experiences God's immense welcome and his openness and goodness towards humanity. In short, the person's broken life begins to make sense, through the spiritual father, as gathered up into an immense, warm heart. This person also begins, by means of the spiritual father, to make out a new image, a more luminous image, without fear of condemnation, without having to cut out any experiences or certain dimensions of character, but in *totality.*

It is precisely this seeing the totality, the wholeness, that is typical of a mind that is enlightened by love, that thinks with love. It is the typical emotion of the discovery of love that triggers the motivating force of conversion, of change, in a person. When a person experiences love, that person's mentality, behavior, and habits all change. It is an experience that does not bind one to the spiritual father, but frees a person into the immense embrace of the true Father because, after all, it is not the spiritual father but the heavenly Father within who loves that person. To be loved is the only way of change, of growth, if we want to use this term, of self-realization, that is not violent, authoritarian, or forced.[41]

Once again I would like to underscore the distinction between this acceptance and a coming to awareness of one's subconscious or repressed experiences by oneself or with a psychotherapist acting according to professional protocols. I do not want to belittle the usefulness of this exercise that certainly is beneficial in achieving a more serene and healthy life. Without doubt, however, it is an entirely different thing to recount one's thoughts, one's dramatic and unsettling stories, to someone who entrusts everything inwardly to God and who, along the way, slowly leads one to the maturity of being capable of independently entrusting these things to God in prayer.

---

41. "Recognizing in love the truth of another, not abstractly, but essentially, transferring in deed the center of our life beyond the limits of our empirical personality, we by so doing reveal and realize our own real truth, our own absolute significance, which consists just in our capacity to transcend the borders of our factual phenomenal being, in our capacity to live not only in ourselves, but also in another. . . . In order genuinely to undermine egoism, it is necessary to oppose to it a love equally concretely specific, permeating the whole of our being and taking possession of everything in it" (Solov'ëv, *The Meaning of Love,* 45-46).

Here we move within, towards an authentic relationship with God in which an awareness at the psychological level takes place, but at the same time these realities are truly assumed by one Person, the God-Father-Love who heals, cleanses, cares for, cures, and brings all to a transfiguration in the resurrection. It is one thing to be intellectually conscious of this and another to add to this knowledge the awareness that everything is not just left behind, but is transfigured in the face of him who showed love on the Cross.

Healing of the Memory

One of the most difficult problems we run up against, as has already been noted, is the problem of memory. This problem is aggravated all the more today by the intense focus on the psyche that we participate in these days. On the one hand, it seems that everything is permissible and that persons mature only by experiencing everything. On the other hand, though, the baggage of unassimilated, unreflected, unspiritualized experiences becomes heavy and weighs upon the conscience.

A "bad memory" exists, a memory of the evil done, of the evil suffered, and even of the evil we have witnessed. It is the warehouse of the memory, both personal as well as collective, that impels towards neurosis, towards a way of acting determined by impulses and motives that escape rationality and self-awareness. Thus people must begin to do everything possible to unfocus, to shift their attention to other things.

Memory, with all its mechanisms, however, continually represents past images, past experiences, and each time it reappears it reawakens a strong charge of negativity, rancor, and aggressiveness. There can also be periods in which it seems that we have neatly organized the past, but only a moment, an encounter, a word, a place, a glance suffices for everything to reemerge. The scars open and the wound reappears even more painfully. We try to busy ourselves with other, more attractive, more meaningful experiences, but the moment they begin to wear out, before moving on to the next best thing, there is always the risk that the memory will make itself felt again.

This memory is thus one that has not been cured or healed. It touches on the whole problem of the collective memory of peoples and nations. In the past it has often happened that nations wounded one another or that many individuals among a people had negative experiences of their contact with other peoples.

The latest period in European history has been characterized, as has been noted, by a humanist-enlightenment culture that washed over Europe with great proclamations, like solidarity, acceptance of differences, peace, etc. Now, however, we witness how all the wounds of long past stories are reemerging. We see that culture satisfied the intellect with "logical exercises," but that it did not take care of the deep levels of humanity.

Now that this fascination with modernity has passed and we are in a time of cultural passage, a whole bad memory, full of scars and unhealed, reemerges, making the way easy for nationalistic movements and incentives for a culture of prejudices and facile judgments of one another to reappear. At the center of Europe, breeding grounds of conflict and even war break out because of an unhealed memory. We can imagine how many conflicts and personal tragedies exist because of an uncleansed personal memory. But what can heal memory? Certainly not forgetfulness or canceling things out. If it were possible to erase every disturbing or oppressive thing with an agonizing emptiness, there would be very little left of some lives.

There must be a way of healing that transforms memory. In the book of Jeremiah it is written: *No longer shall they teach one another, or say to each other, "Know the LORD," for they shall all know me, from the least of them to the greatest, says the LORD; for I will forgive their iniquity, and remember their sin no more* (Jer. 31:34). People today have a great need to meet someone who accepts everything they have to say without asking where they have been, what they have done, where they have failed. They need someone who reassures them, preparing a feast for them similar to that of the father for the prodigal son, no longer remembering his sin. They need another person who tells them in a strong and authentic relationship that their iniquity will no longer be remembered.

This does not mean that the sins are simply cancelled out, that their iniquity is forgotten, but rather it means that he who forgives you remembered you with love even while you were sinning. It means that sin does not mark the minutes and acts of your life, but that your life — including the past — becomes a perpetual metamorphosis, a perpetual openness to him. Thus, what was a bad memory, an act or an episode that persecuted and disturbed your heart, becomes a beautiful memory in that it recalls the One who has forgiven you. From evil you pass into the Person of Goodness and of Mercy. In the New Testament, the most profound knowledge of God is the knowledge that comes through forgiveness.[42]

Those who have experienced forgiveness never again forget the One who forgave them. Rather, reached out to by and united to him in love, there is no longer any force that can separate them from him, not even martyrdom (cf. Rom. 8:35). A spiritual father must be the image of him who is Mercy and who forgives, in such a way that, by means of forgiveness and the discovery of the true image of God, people might change and grow in an ever more complete life. The culmination of Christian pedagogy is forgiveness because in forgiving even the things that are furthest from God, those things most closed to any spiritual meaning, become spiritual, become an everlasting remembrance of and communion with him.

Helping the Encounter between Humanity and God

In this way, preparing the existential encounter between a person and God, a spiritual father is an aid. His personal relationship is certainly a privileged element of this encounter. Nevertheless, precisely because he offers only the space favorable to everything taking place, such an encounter proves itself in the measure in which he, offering a relationship, is at the same time reserved.

---

42. Cf. Silvano Fausti, *Ricorda e racconta il Vangelo: La catechesi narrativa di Marco* (Recalling and Recounting the Gospel: The Narrative Catechesis in Mark) (Milan: Ancora, 1989), 466.

A spiritual father can only verify, by observing the signs that are glimpsed in the person who comes to meet with him, whether that person has a true religious principle, not a spiritual illusion or a mental or psychological fixation that makes the person believe God is present while in effect the person is completely locked in the psyche to the point of never emerging from the ego. A spiritual father is the test of the characteristics that accompany a person moved by the Holy Spirit.

Given that the most frequent deviations and psychological sicknesses are tested in the encounter with God, it is precisely to these moments that the true quality of a spiritual father can be traced back. A spiritual father is aware that the relationship between humanity and God is real, founded on that real link which is love, the only reality that unites and does not confuse or create rivals, or lead to exclusivity. That is why the spiritual father observes whether the person is truly docile to the Holy Spirit who pours into our hearts the love of God the Father (cf. Rom. 5:5), or rather, who affirms the will of the person who has decided to be good, faithful, believing, prayerful, etc.

Given that the goal of the spiritual life is the acquisition of the Holy Spirit,[43] in order that he might enliven, illuminate, and guide us in every action and every intention, a clear sign of true spiritual growth is this docility to the Spirit. It is, therefore, not stubbornness, not forcefully defending one's own will and opinion, but having an openness to considering the other. In fact, we have seen that this attention to the other is a religious principle.

The spiritual person is therefore a person of faith, a person who considers God, his word, and his way of acting. Humility is the true and sure criterion to which a spiritual father is attentive. Humility is both docility as well as seeing oneself deprived of a solid point within oneself, a recog-

43. "Prayer, fasting, vigil and all other Christian practices, however good they may be in themselves, do not constitute the aim of our Christian life, although they serve as the indispensable means of reaching this end. The true aim of our Christian life consists in the acquisition of the HOLY SPIRIT OF GOD. As for fasts, and vigils, and prayer, and almsgiving, and every good deed done for Christ's sake, they are only means of acquiring the Holy Spirit of God" (St. Seraphim of Sarov, *Spiritual Instructions,* vol. 1 of *Little Russian Philokalia* [Ouzinkie, AK: St. Herman Press, 1991], 86).

nition of the one firm and sure point in the other person, or rather, in the love between the two.[44]

That enthrallment in the love of God that bears fruit in love towards oneself and others occurs in spiritual fatherhood. One begins to look upon oneself and others with a gaze of "togetherness," to the point of seeing the movement of the Spirit even in the spheres furthest from that which can be immediately recognized as religious. This reasoning of love that begins to condition the entire way of thinking and behaving is found in the narrowest sphere in which the person lives. In fact, the person who has truly met God in love and has begun to orient life toward him also begins to understand, in love, one's own defects, and the darkest parts of oneself.[45]

44. "I see clearly that I would not find even an atom resembling at least the seed of autonomous, true, and eternal being in the personality and its multiform manifestations that I claim. I am the seed, dead in the earth, but the seed's death is the condition for its return to life. God will raise me up because he is with me. I know him in me as a dark, creating womb. I know him in me as something eternally superior to me that always surpasses that in me which is the best and the holiest. I know him in me as the living principle of being, infinitely more vast than I am, and therefore containing, along with others, my forces and attributes, even the attribute of personal consciousness that pertains to me. From him I am, and he remains in me, and if he does not abandon me he will even create other forms of his presence in me, that is, my personality. God not only created me but creates me without stopping and will continue creating me. He certainly desires that I also further create him in me as up until now I have created him. There can be no descent without willing acceptance. In a sense, the two acts have the same value, the one who welcomes becomes equal in dignity to him who descends into them. God cannot abandon me if I do not abandon him. The law of love, inscribed in our hearts (because we read its invisible characters effortlessly) proclaims that the psalmist was right in saying to God: '. . . You will not abandon my soul to the nether world, nor will you suffer your faithful one to undergo corruption' (Ps. 16:10)" (Vjačeslav Ivanov, *Perepiska iz dvuch uglov*, in *Sobranie Sočinenii*, vol. 3 [Brussels, 1921], translated into Italian as *Corrispondenza da un angolo all'altro* [Correspondence from One Corner to Another] [Milan, 1976], 38). Ivanov further affirms: "Two people who love each other encounter one another in such a way that, in the same moment, a third person is present between them as well — the loving God himself — 'Even a third is present, and that third one is love'" (*Mysli o simvolizme* [Thoughts on Symbolism], in *Sobranie Sočinenii* [Brussels, 1921], 3.606).

45. Cf. André Louf, *Tuning in to Grace: The Quest for God*, tr. John Vriend, (Kalamazoo, MI: Cistercian Publications, 1992).

On a social level, this is in love for one's enemies.[46] If a spiritual father allows one to entrust oneself to God in the heart, one experiences an ever greater freedom. A spiritual father is a person of freedom and the one who goes to him becomes such as well. This is not just freedom "from" or even just freedom "for," but a freedom "with," to be free with God and with others. On a psychological level, this guarantees a healthy spiritual fatherhood, free from every wrong, constricting, or conditioned bondage.

Some Risks to Avoid

A spiritual father cannot substitute for Christ. He cannot even guarantee that the person feels welcomed, with the psychological effects that come from that. He cannot substitute for the Holy Spirit or guide the thoughts of another step by step. He cannot be the light that illuminates the other. This would be a sure path to a pathological dependence on himself, a real stumbling block to the growth of faith. Today, a spiritual father does not demand that the person do what he says but that the person listen and prayerfully consider what he says and arrive at a decision, which could even be the complete opposite of his counsel. His task is to propose a spiritual thought for the other to consider so that through this process the other's mentality might mature. Woe be it if he introduces his thought in place of the other's. Only the path of discernment and a truly spiritual relationship can avoid this risk.

Another frequent error is found in being moved by the suffering person to the point of offering an exquisitely human, psychological, and paternal consolation. This also leads others to a dependency on the spiritual father, making him into an idol. The spiritual father cannot substitute for the Paraclete, the only true Consoler.

Another risk to avoid is entering into discussion with the other in a dialectic manner, because, again, the person concentrates on the spiritual father, on what he says or thinks, instead of on God and on his word. In short, it is necessary to avoid every behavior that may misdirect the person toward

46. Cf. Archimandrite Sophrony (Sakharov), *St. Silouan the Athonite,* 116.

the spiritual father and away from God. In the same way the spiritual father cannot be easily offended by the person who comes to him either because this is also a refined system of bondage, of making one dependent.

Perhaps the most frequent obstacle is that of investigating into the person's past, becoming snared in looking for causes. A spiritual father does not overlook the past, nevertheless he places more attention on its spiritual significance and helps to see the past in the light of salvation, in the light of the Love of God. Above all, he seeks to orient the person toward a realistic future, toward moving forward. This might seem a small thing, but in Europe, which by now has become a senile continent showing signs of reverting to the past, openness to the future, to hope, and to eschatology are urgently necessary realities.

A Reality That Is Attractive Today

If we remember the first lines of this reflection, we can already understand just how spiritual fatherhood is that which can help contemporary persons return to the truth. Spiritual fatherhood consists in completely opening the space of love to interpersonal relations. It is a caring and attentive accompaniment of the other. "The new evangelization, to which John Paul II continually calls us, consists above all in the accompanying of those who are cut off from the witness of love. It means accompanying those people on the journey, which is not a casual thing but leads, through the inner logic of Christian love itself, to a full confession of faith and belonging to the Church."[47]

When I speak of spiritual fatherhood, therefore, I am not just thinking of a specific charism in the Church or of professionally formed spiritual guides; rather I am mainly referring to what has been handed down to us from the ancient tradition of spiritual fatherhood as the spiritual-theological structure. This reveals to us that the Church is most of all a world of relationships so strong in Christ that they are even capable of personalizing things and institutions.

47. Conferenze Episcopale Italiana, *Evangelizzazione e testimonianza della carità* (Evangelization and Witness of Charity), 10.

This means that the person, in the proper dimension of love, is the likeness of God and that God can speak to humanity and reveal himself precisely in relationships. Spiritual fatherhood introduces people to healthy relationships, where they begin, above all in forgiveness, to walk the way of love that with its interior logic leads to Christ, to the image of that God who is an eternal and perfect "community" of Three.

Spiritual fatherhood helps us to avoid various dualisms, especially that of distinguishing and separating theology, reflection, from the content that is personally lived by a person. "Christian truth is not an abstract theory. It is above all the living person of the Lord Jesus Christ (John 14:6) who, risen, lives among his own (cf. Matt. 18:20; Luke 24:13-35). This is why the truth can be heard, understood, and communicated only within a complete and vital experience that is personal and in communion, that is concrete and practical, and in which the awareness of truth finds its match in authentic life."[48]

Spiritual fatherhood is not a technique or a pastoral "system" but rather is that apostolic activity that is already a typical message of our faith in the world. Spiritual fatherhood is a "method" that at the same time is the revelation of the content of our faith.

4. Some Suggestions for a Concrete Encounter

Pray While Listening

A spiritual father seeks to guard that openness to God in his heart, to guard that remembrance of God that is constantly a giving precedence to him. He should remain in the typically religious attitude of prayer, when, that is, prayer becomes an attitude. I advise maintaining this attitude during direction sessions, repeating in the heart what is being heard and relating it to God. Thus it is possible to remain in prayer and to avoid the harshest risk, that of feeling oneself a protagonist, of beginning to think of what one should say, that is, of treating the other as an object of study,

---

48. Ibid., 9.

of investigation. Moreover, this is how to fulfill the role of mediator, communicating and entrusting the life that is being heard to God. It is in this way that a spiritual father introduces communion into that procession, a communion into which the other is invited.

Do Not Judge

Since he does not yet know the person except from what has been said, instead of drawing conclusions from what he has heard, the spiritual father can choose another way, for example, agreeing on some small exercise for a determined amount of time — a reading for example — at the end of which it can be tested, based on what was agreed upon and only on that basis, whether it is proper to clearly express observations to the other. For example, if this person is lazy, the spiritual father can, based on mutual agreement, begin a dialog on laziness. If however he were to do it based on what the person said about his or her past, it could quickly take on a sense of accusation and non-acceptance.

This method of proceeding is even more positive if it concerns healing a person's notable defects. In fact, pointing out these defects when they surface during the agreed-upon time together, one does not fixate the person on the past as would occur if they were pointed out only on the basis of what was heard. In this latter case, the person would be focused on the negative, which for the most part the person is already aware of but feels unable to change. Thus the person's sense of guilt and frustration would be heightened.

5. The Danger of Spiritual Fathers and of Spiritual Readings

The new generations continuously deny being dependent on anyone. We know that one of the fundamental rules of liberal ideology is that of creating a refusal of any obedience, except obviously toward liberal publicity itself, which should not be conditioned by anyone. In this way, liberalism can rule over people. We see a particular tragedy in the fact that those most vulnerable to this can be the youth of ex-communist regimes.

Certainly, some dramatic conditionings of the past regimes are still at work. Notwithstanding this, it is necessary to admit that this problem has strongly blocked the development of the Church in those countries. Many young people actually deny the experience of their older fellow citizens. They rely on many foreign superficial, liberal "theologies" while believing themselves autonomous. Obviously, they are not aware of the trap in which they find themselves and which they will regret later because of the years that they are thus losing.

The essence of this liberalistic trap consists of the fact that they are abandoning themselves to pride and spiritual vainglory. It becomes more important to be autonomous than to fulfill the will of God. This type of rebellion completely blocks youth in their growth and their creativity and often even leads them to psychological problems. Everything becomes difficult. They are mostly struck in their relationships with people, where, because of an absolute uncertainty in themselves, they seek continuous confirmation and recognition. They therefore usually enclose themselves in groups with similar people having similar difficulties. In these circles they are incapable of creativity, finding only a negative complaining and a regurgitation of their own destiny that they have created by themselves.

These young people are exposed to many possible manipulations. The trap consists of the fact that they think themselves autonomous and creative but in the end they all wind up the same. These young people choose the same forms of rebellion, of disagreement, and of self-assertion.

All these phenomena show that the person who is not already open to interior certitude and therefore who does not know the Father, becomes the bait for many temptations. Such persons very quickly choose a stepfather, one who later torments and depersonalizes them.

What does all that mean? If in 1968 famous thinkers preached the denial of mothers and fathers and tradition, and even the killing of teachers, today we witness such an urgent need for a father, a teacher, an ideal, that there is the risk of following in an irrational, infantile, directionless manner anyone who presents a certain authority. Since we are in the era of publicity where the rule of the best and the quickest reigns, we are blinded by results with little sense of the burden of the task. We thus skip steps, and little ones are given food and drink that is too strong. In time this can lead to a complete rejection of everything religious.

To imitate a master in some things that are the fruit of a long asceticism and of much grace can mean spiritual suicide for the beginner. It means not understanding what the religious principle is, but creating for oneself, with reason and the will, a religious world within one's own purely immanent horizon, a world that is evidently completely false.[49]

On the other hand, as heirs of a rationalist, conceptual culture — that nevertheless remains idealistic in its structure — we sometimes think that masters are not needed, that it is enough to read and to think. This road leads instead to an inevitable dualism, and consequently, to a fatigue, a discouragement, and thus to an abandonment of the road that was undertaken.[50]

Conclusion

In these few pages I have tried to highlight how, in a world impoverished in respect to all that pertains to the person, to the personal, and to relationship, the art of spiritual fatherhood can represent the space of recovery of a healthy relationship and therefore of the possibility of entering into the way of knowing God as a living Person and as Love. In a world

49. "Whoever tries to pray only on the basis of what they have heard said or have learned gets lost just as one who has no guide" (Gregory the Sinaite, in *La filocalia,* ed. M. B. Artioli and M. F. Lovato [Turin: Gribaudi, 1985], 601).

50. Regarding the anxiety provoked in a young monk on reading Evagrius's *Kephalaia Gnostika,* see Barsanuphius and John of Gaza, Epistle 600, in *Barsenuphe et Jean de Gaza, Correspondance,* tr. Lucien Regnault and Philippe LeMaire (Solesmes: Abbaye Saint-Pierre de Solesmes, 1971), 391-394. "The holy fathers refer to many that had set themselves to practicing prayer incorrectly, following methods for which they were neither mature nor capable enough and who fell into spiritual blindness and were disturbed by mental anxieties" (Ignatiy Briančaninov, *Sočinenja Episkopa Ignatija* (St. Petersburg, 1905), translated into Italian as *Preghiera e lotta spirituale* (Prayer and Spiritual Struggle) (Turin: Gribaudi, 1991), 146. At the risk of being near to the great masters and imitating them in their asceticism without being at their level of spiritual life, cf ibid., 146-147.

characterized by the absence of a true religious way of thinking, spiritual fatherhood, precisely because of its fundamental attitude, which is that of recognizing the other and of taking the Holy Spirit into account, can become the sphere of an authentic religious experience.

In a world in which we risk remaining immature and superficial because of continual distractions, spiritual fatherhood can help us achieve the continual deepening and maturity that is expressed in charity and in discernment. In a world that easily leads to individualism and subjectivism, spiritual fatherhood can lead us to an acceptance of the objectivity of life. Contemporary people, locked within their own subjectivism, can only open up again if they are included in an interpersonal relationship. Even the overshadowing of reason, described at the beginning of this article, will pass away when people come into relationship with the other and when the desire for communication rises in them once again. We will have a renewal of the intellect when it is woven into interpersonal relationships where it will be illuminated by love.

Nevertheless, humanity will continue to create apparent objectivities and unconditioned existences for itself. In fact, it is only in relationship that it can come to the knowledge of the other as an autonomous reality, absolute in itself whether or not one thinks it so. Without this discovery of objectivity, humanity is a menace to itself. The incapacity to know objectivity means that, sooner or later, even every thought of objectivity becomes a merely abstract thought, incapable of seriously taking objectivity into account. Without the capacity of objective reflection every civil society, every agreement, and every law is undermined because the human being as a being of relationship and of love is undermined.

A culture that does not have a true knowledge of objectivity is in reality not a culture because it is not a dialog of communication. An objectivity that is not based on a vital content is only a rational construct under the pretext of objectivity, capriciously sustained by science. Objectivity, which is based on the living reality of an absolute person, is a real objectivity because it must take the dimension of freedom typical of the agapic principle into consideration. Until we recognize the objectivity of the free existence of the other, we cannot truly speak of objectivity but only of our, more or less clever, mental constructs. Only objectivity that is so personal as to be free is true objectivity. It is true because reason can neither control nor understand it with its logic of deduction.

The recognition of freedom and of unpredictability is, in fact, the recognition of the objectivity of the other. We can arrive at the knowledge of this free dimension of the other, which can save us from terrifying, random causality by means of an intelligence that knows, thanks to love, within relationship. Otherwise, we will be thrown into a random game and will be locked in our own inner world of contrary passions and of causality: in the circle of the personal life of families or their surrogates, where the other will never be a reality except in a flight of fantasy; in sociopolitical life, where the only objectivity will be individualistic interest masked by a thick veil of cordial phrases and convincing humanistic affirmations; in international politics, where the reciprocal recognition and accord among peoples consists in a dangerous fantasy of economic intrigues rather than in attention to the reality of the other.

This is the reason why spiritual fatherhood leads us to the Church, orients us toward community, and creates us for community. It helps us accept the Church and live in her who acts in history and in concrete life. This means a real rebirth of humanity and culture in all its dimensions, from science to art, from philosophy to a simple, social living together. Relationship, understood against the background of the Trinity, cannot be confused with the intimate relativity of two people who look upon each other. Every relationship is true if it is opened to the Church, to universal humanity, and to the Triune God.